# Successful Football Betting

www.bestbetbooks.co.uk

**Cover by Pure Design, Shrewsbury**

First published 2002 by

Aesculus Press Limited
PO Box 307
Crewe
Cheshire
CW3 0WA

Typeset on an Apple Macintosh
by Aesculus Press using QuarkXpress

Printed and bound in Great Britain by MFP Design & Print, Manchester

1-904328-01-6

# contents

# preface

Never in my time at Ladbrokes, Sky Sports or *Sportsadviser* magazine, have I met someone with a better knowledge of football betting than Geoff Harvey. Over the last two years, through his weekly column in *Sportsadviser*, Geoff has uncovered countless betting loopholes that have had the country's bookmakers running scared.

Successful Football Betting looks at football betting from innovative angles and explores the opportunities, as well as the pitfalls in the battle against the bookie. Geoff explores all aspects of football betting, from punishing out-of-line quotes from the big firms to finding value opportunities on the person-to-person betting exchanges. With analytical expertise and specialisation that the football odds compilers can only dream of, Geoff continually manages to stay one step ahead of the bookmakers.

Far from being a dry, analytical account of how to take on the layers, Geoff has produced a fascinating and entertaining guide on how to make money from the national game. While the majority of punters fall down by continually trying to predict match results, Geoff thrives on football's unpredictability and specialises in finding when the obvious is NOT going to happen.

With the advent of tax-free betting, unlimited information on the internet and the fierce competition between new and established bookmakers, there has never been a better time to bet on football.

**Ed Chamberlain - presenter on Sky Sports'**
**90 Minutes and editor of Sportsadviser**

8 . successful football betting

# introduction

It was while lolling about on a bench in the picture book village of Modbury in Devon, on a sweltering Sunday morning in 1993, that I made a discovery which was to turn my interest in football betting into something of an all-consuming obsession.

Squinting at the minuscule type of the Australian football (soccer) results in the *Mail on Sunday*, I began scrawling the scores on the corresponding William Hill football coupon. Going down the list, a definite pattern emerged. There were 12 matches where the away team was offered at odds in the region of 5-4. They had all won. I made a mental note of this and started to fantasise that maybe, just maybe, this could be the big one.

To be honest, it wasn't exactly the first time I thought I'd stumbled across an ingenious, fail-safe method of permanently ensuring a profit from football betting. A few years earlier, during a particularly professionally unproductive spell working the evening shift in a petrol station, my boss and I, over large hunks of pizza, scribbled out mad staking plans on blank credit card dockets.

I distinctly remember him proclaiming "I'll have to sell my house to raise the stake money" on discovering there was a fiendish combination of correct score bets that appeared to guarantee vast riches. Had he done so, he might today have been propped up in a doorway with a bottle of surgical spirit - because, oddly, the system didn't work.

But the Australian football business seemed as though it could be the real thing. Within a few weeks I had completed a page of an exercise book, with 16 columns of scores arranged in price brackets from 'under 1-2', through '6-4' and

'2-1', moving towards the other extreme of 'greater than 8-1'. I was able to take a rough and ready look at the consequences of backing away teams in each price bracket. Although a number of price brackets made a loss, many racked up an enormous notional profit, particularly those around 6-4.

Betting on matches in the State Australian football leagues is only offered for the three months of the British close season, so it was a long wait until I could see whether I'd stumbled upon a bookie-busting system or was simply witnessing a short-term blip in the fortunes of away teams. To my relief, and some astonishment, the theory wasn't reduced to tatters as soon as I started wagering hard cash. Picking seven away teams (covering them with 35 trebles) at odds between Evens and 2-1, the winnings started to flow.

During the following seasons, the tattered yellow exercise book was ditched in favour of A4 files stuffed with coupons, calculations and computer printouts. Australian football betting information began to take over the flat, and was only kept under control by my wife's efforts to keep each week's stats in manageable bundles, neatly labelled.

By 1997, I seemed to have found the optimum way of combining away team selections - covering nine matches in different price brackets with trebles. Although my stakes were not in the professional league, the profit was running consistently between 40-60 per cent over each three-month season.

In seven years, I became something of a specialist in the location of William Hill branches (for security reasons they are not listed in the phone book). Fearing that at any moment I'd be rumbled, causing Hills to lower the heaven sent prices on away teams, I placed endless coupons in small denominations of rarely more than £30 a time. 'Auscoup' (pronounced *Oz-coo*), as my wife and I unimaginatively named the exercise, still had legs six years later.

But in 1999 the weekly betting paper *Racing & Football Outlook* seemed to be catching up fast. Within their excellent articles on Australian football, it was becoming clear they were beginning to suspect that something was up with the away prices, particularly Hills.

By this time I'd found a number of other strategies that were paying off, so fearing *Racing & Football Outlook* were going to spell it out in black and white, I bashed out a piece for my column in *Sportsadviser* magazine in June 2000 under the title 'Bookies don't give a XXXX'. I hoped readers may be able to take advantage before the whole thing collapsed completely.

By a strange coincidence Hills didn't offer Australian coupons that summer. The game was up. In fact, having discovered the Aussie loophole, the next few came thick and fast. As a result, throughout the last three years, I've been involved in a bit of a cat and mouse game with the major firms, having to hint strongly in pieces I've written that an opportunity exists, when I knew full well that there was a glaring error in pricing.

Some loopholes were closed down immediately on publication (particularly where they involved Ladbrokes); others remain joyously open. Many, including new ones available at the time of writing, are described later on. Much of the material here is significantly different from previous publications on the subject of football betting.

I have avoided endless reams of football statistics unless they are specifically useful in explaining how there is a betting advantage to be had. Similarly, I have only a passing interest in traditional 'prediction' systems. We know that if Manchester United play Southampton at Old Trafford, there is a rather strong possibility of a home win.

Too frequently in football-betting writing there is a long technical analysis that presents a conclusion we could have arrived at in five seconds. I don't want to present facts simply reflecting that the bookies have posted the correct odds. "As usual the bookies have got their sums right" is a phrase I hope to avoid.

Unless I have a particularly large wager, the actual result of an individual bet is sometimes of secondary interest. When I place any bet, I try to have a figure in mind as to the extent of my advantage. Placing bets on certain types of matches to be draws on Ladbrokes half-time coupon (prior to them changing the odds in early 2001) yielded a net profit of around eight per cent.

Translated into multiple bets (using trebles to cover eight selections), the profit rose to around 35 per cent long-term. The result on an individual Saturday, while not exactly irrelevant, did not change the fundamental fact that there was an advantage in the favour of the backer. Unless there was a sudden change in the way football was being played, a profit was eventually assured.

The fundamental principle is: do the odds available give a fair reflection of the chance of an event happening? This is critically different from asking a question like, "Will Luton win today?"

Just as chronic, obsessive gambling is by definition a destructive habit, successful betting does have its liberating aspects. In life, most of us are shackled by being judged by others in both direct and indirect ways. We get exam results, appraisals at work, and others form impressions of us on the basis of scant evidence. Football betting is a strangely pure intellectual activity. You simply sit in front of a coupon and at the end of deliberations come up with a simple set of

1's, 2's and X's. Regardless of which technique you use to make selections, if you put them in the wrong place you're inviting a spiral of financial decline. Shove them in the right places consistently and you possess a highly sought after and socially useful betting skill - that of being able to produce cash more or less at will, without having to get your hands grubby. No-one will give you a certificate - your performance is measured by the state of your betting bank.

To profit from football betting requires a rather odd set of characteristics. In fact I've yet to meet the 'perfect' football punter. An encyclopaedic knowledge of the game helps - something I admit I don't possess. I know seemingly obscure stuff like the frequency of away wins in the first round of the League Cup, but ask me to reel off the names of the current Coventry squad and I'd be struggling. Football super-brains have a fantastic recall of facts, but knowing that Crewe play at Gresty Road doesn't have a great deal of use for betting purposes.

A smattering of maths knowledge is useful, though the area of statistics that relates to betting is fairly specialised. A lot of gambling stats revolve around the relatively obscure subject of binomials, a branch of statistics that tells us, for instance, we need 35 trebles to cover seven selections. A lot of calculations are based around 'measures of central tendency' - means, modes and the like. Using them correctly is particularly important as many bookmakers have shown themselves to be vulnerable in this area.

Having little interest in maths for its own sake, I have developed just about enough knowledge to get by - though I often turn to others, better qualified, to explain patiently things they probably see as rather basic.

British horse racing's byzantine rules and immersion in internal politics are unlikely to prove a match for the lure of a game so universally loved and understood that it now seems an anachronism that racing has clung on to its majority betting market share for so long. Gradually, online betting firms are concentrating exclusively on football.

Any detailed discussion of the current state of internet betting, though, is bound to go out of date as soon as the ink dries. At the turn of the 21st century, just 10 years after its baptism, there are signs the online industry may have reached critical mass. But the internet has ensured that vast amounts of information on every minority interest, from windsurfing through football betting to polymer technology, is now circulated.

In each of the subject areas, coverage has expanded so rapidly that it has, in some ways, made redundant the term 'expert'. Doctors are alarmed that the internet allows patients to accumulate a greater knowledge of their conditions than any professional would have the time to gather. A similar situation exists for bookie's odds compilers. They have to spread themselves relatively thinly. There are people out there, hiding behind their internet aliases, who do little but study the pattern of corners and bookings in football matches.

Unlike bookmakers, we don't have to keep track of vast numbers of matches, find out why a client's account has been miscredited, or worry about public relations. Time and the ability to be selective are our greatest assets. This effectively means that football betting professionals are in a position to be more 'professional' than the firms they are trying to take money off. If, 20 years ago, punters had been dangled the carrot of a level playing field with bookies, we would have thought it was an unreachable goal.

But I wouldn't want to give the impression that good betting is a robotic, detached activity. I am lucky to have a close circle of friends who, having been worn down over the years, have had little choice but to cultivate an interest in gambling. I love the homework that comes with football betting but I also actively participate in the riots breaking out in my sitting room as two quick goals go our way.

Many books on gambling are advertised along the lines of 'a good general guide'. This really isn't one of them. I assume a fair amount of knowledge on the reader's part. For instance, it is generally customary not to swap to-and-fro between fixed-odds and spread betting.

I've guessed that by now most people remotely interested in gambling will know how spread betting works. So the subject suddenly intrudes, without warning, into the text. Similarly I launch into a discussion of areas such as over-rounds without much preliminary explanation.

A lot of gambling writing can be a little tentative. There is talk of 'potentially useful strategies' and 'possible avenues to explore'. I have tried not to litter the book with disclaimers. If I think there is something definitely worthwhile in a strategy then I've included it; if not, I've left it out. For this reason I have steered clear of areas where I have no particular view or knowledge.

I know from experience that gamblers get very heated when they debate their favourite subject. In many areas I've simply stuck my head above the parapet and will wait for the volley of incoming fire.

If I haven't said something that you vehemently disagree with, then I have probably not succeeded in my aim of setting out ideas that will be quite new to a lot of readers. If I have, then my only plea is - we're supposed to be on the same side!

## 14 . successful football betting

To enjoy profits at football betting frequently requires the punter to look at everything in an upside-down, inside-out sort of way. In fact, if you always find yourself out of step with everything that others are thinking, you are probably treading the right path already.

chapter **one**

# measuring punting performance

Leaf through the pages of any of the racing or betting press and you will be assaulted by the adverts trumpeting the various claims of tipsters. Like most commercial enterprises, some are quite good, others are nothing but charlatans. Note the way in which their claims are presented. Any that talk about strike-rates can usually be consigned to the 'completely bogus' pile.

Claiming that 53 per cent of bets are winners is meaningless. If all the bets were at 8-1, then it is a phenomenal performance. If, which is much more likely, they were mostly a motley bunch of 1-2 shots, then it's a performance that is worse than what you could have achieved by picking bets at random. Similarly, more often with racing than football, we are presented with an over-long list of winners' prices - '10-1, 16-1 and more this month alone!' Again there is nothing to assess. If you put a couple of quid on every single competitor or result, then it's really a doddle to find winners at huge prices.

The only acceptable way to judge betting performance is to use exactly the same system as the bookies when they rate your individual betting ability. What they want to know is, if you have spent £500 betting, how much have you retained, including your returned stake money? This is then expressed as a percentage of your stake. If you spent £500 and were returned £750, then you have a 'performance' of 150 per cent; £500 spent and £400 back - an 80 per cent performance, and so on.

If you were simply to bet on a large number of football matches (in singles) purely at random, then you are going to fall prey to the bookies' margin over time. So, in the long run, you are liable to lose just over 10 per cent of every pound you stake, as their margin is just over 10 per cent on each match. In fact, high street bookies have been returning only around 60 per cent of stakes for many years, as a vast majority of football bettors line up whopping accumulator bets, in hope of an occasional big win.

There is still a huge mass of such punters in shops up and down the land; but as fast as they are contributing to the high street profits, there are more clued up high-rolling customers who are gobbling up the best prices and forcing down overall margins. Without using any particular skill it is possible to increase performance levels to well over 90 per cent. If you are betting exclusively on football matches where you are taking a best (or at least better than average) price, you are clearly eroding the theoretical margin in the bookies' favour.

With spread betting, an individual's performance can simply be expressed as the amount won as a percentage of the amount lost. Broadly, the overall margins in spread betting are similar to those with the fixed-odds - though with the spread companies more inclined to offer markets which cannot be directly compared to similar markets of their competitors, it is increasingly difficult to shop around for the best spread betting prices.

In general, however, the calculation produces roughly the same outcome. With spread betting you should, by chance alone, lose a little more than 10 per cent of your total stakes. With both forms of betting, the huge task is to haul yourself into the idyllic world of the 100 per cent plus performance bracket, where you are consistently winning slightly more than you are staking. The difference between a 99 per cent performance and a 101 per cent performance is small in numerical terms, but there is psychological chasm between someone who is slightly up long-term and one who is slightly down.

Of course it would take an eternity for one person to settle on an exact percentage performance figure, and anyway circumstances and betting patterns may change radically. But let's assume it was possible to pin one person to a precise performance figure. At 99 per cent, the more you stake the more you must lose. The opposite is true once you surmount the hurdle of 100 per cent. Suddenly, the more money you can pile on the more you must win. The professional tactic, therefore, is to pile on the cash and let a small margin in their favour produce a financial return that repays the time and effort. Or at least they try to pile it on.

This leads directly to the knotty subject of having bets 'knocked back' - i.e. bets accepted only at lesser odds, or bets accepted at a smaller stake than required, or simply not being accepted at all. Until quite recently bookmakers have been tight-lipped about the subject, virtually denying that it ever happens. In many ways, it's a fair fight. Anyone walking into the same shop every day and casually walking off with wads of their cash is a little naive to believe the situation can last indefinitely.

In fact a brief look at the economics of bookmakers with high street premises almost makes you have sympathy with them. A football punter who places large single bets (even if he does so more or less at random, with no appreciable skill factor) is likely to be unable to produce enough profit for the shop to make his custom worthwhile, since they have to pay the fixed costs of running the business.

The bookies core business is the crowd of generally older clientele with their through-the-card forecast doubles on the greyhounds, or the majority of football bettors who are trying to use their football coupons to generate a lottery-type win. Such customers pose no danger to their bookies, since they probably only win back around 60 per cent of their stakes. But when the performance level of a customer reaches much above 90 per cent, he becomes as welcome as a shoplifter in a department store. Those placing bets regularly at the same high street bookmaker are the most likely to have a bet turned down.

In theory a shop is supposed to monitor all clients to ensure none of them are permitted to get ahead long-term. It's not that winning customers are turned away as such. If you are a basically a losing customer who has a freak large win, you're not suddenly going to find bets turned down. However, customers who are consistently in profit are soon politely asked to take their business elsewhere, - or, less drastically, have their permitted stakes reduced.

The situation with telephone and internet accounts is both better and worse at the same time. Because these operations are cheaper to run they are, in theory, somewhat more tolerant of winning accounts. But of course, unlike the high street shops, the firms know precisely what your performance rating is. With a handful of companies on the internet, the problem of having stakes reduced is reaching absurd levels. There are tales of account holders who are only slightly ahead long-term having tiny bets of less than £30 knocked back.

The spread firms are particularly tolerant, as it is comparatively easy for them to adjust prices to balance their books. There are figures bandied about that they will allow clients to get ahead by sums of £40,000 before they start turning the screw. However, they don't tolerate anyone attempting arbitrage frequently. It might be difficult to get away with a mere £500 advantage at a high street bookie. Here, the new forms of betting exchanges have a decisive advantage. As they take a commission on each trade they are completely disinterested in the performance level of the individual client.

At this point you may well ask about the performance rating of the bloke whose book you are patiently reading. In terms of staking, I am not the highest roller on the planet - with stakes varying anywhere between £60 and £1,500. On straightforward football bets assessed as singles, where I am simply betting on match results, my performance rating is not especially spectacular at 106 per cent - not enough to make a profit when formerly paying tax on singles, but sufficient to get ahead on multiple bets.

However, many of my wagers are placed on the basis of pricing mistakes, which boosts my overall performance to its current 116 per cent. But I know that many of the opportunities are quite fleeting, so it is not a performance rating I can guarantee into the future. Where definite loopholes appear to exist, I am particularly keen not to place bets on account - not because I am scared they will close me down for getting ahead, but so they cannot find out what I'm doing and discover the error that exists in their prices.

The result is that I hardly ever use accounts in my own name, and simply get bets on by calling on the goodwill of a variety of friends with accounts. I am forever travelling short but time-consuming distances to place bets on the high street. London, not surprisingly, is good betting territory as the concentration of betting shops is very high. My performance from one shop to the other varies wildly. I know I am around £8,000 up on one particular shop in rural South-East England, but considerably down in another close to my home.

The advantage of spreading stakes around thinly is that they never see you long enough to get an impression of whether you're ahead and consequently don't look too closely at winning coupons. The concept of a performance rating based around the 100 per cent return figure is also useful in testing out whether there is any mileage in a particular theory or system. Say you thought the 0-0 scoreline was over-priced in European games. The most effective way of seeing whether this is the case is to look at the consequence of backing all games in this category to be 0-0 to a £1 stake.

By looking at the over-round built into correct score prices it is straightforward to deduce that backing any scoreline at random will only return around 70 per cent of stakes. If the 0-0 draw returns more than this over a large sample of matches, then there may be some evidence that the result is undervalued in comparison to other scorelines. If the overall return exceeds 100 per cent of stakes, then you could be on to something.

chapter **two**

# breaking the tax barrier

It is slightly strange that football betting, of all things, finds itself in the centre of a debate about how nation states have the right to govern, and tax, their inhabitants. Serious football bettors are the unlikely beneficiaries of a medium - the internet - which has no respect for international boundaries, tax regimes, or regional moral codes. In Britain, the duty payable on stakes, enforced for generations, was little more than the Government's 'punishment' to punters for indulging in what has generally been seen as an idle leisure pursuit.

When Nigel Lawson abolished on-course racing duty in 1987, it signalled clearly that the interests of the racing and betting industry were part of the Governments concerns. This was a significant shift in focus towards acceptance of betting as a perfectly respectable pastime. It is difficult to imagine ministers publicly talking of helping the tobacco industry in the same way - and yet the indirect tax regimes imposed on both cigarettes and gambling to that point suggests that they were both officially considered vices to roughly the same extent.

Having gained considerable respectability, the subtle and successful lobbying effort by the bookmaking industry to get into the UK Government's good books, was suddenly and dramatically taken out of both parties' hands. The realisation that the internet offered the opportunity for anyone in the world to place a bet online with anyone else in the world, meant that individual nations became powerless to prevent its citizens from gambling. But, more critically, it rendered them equally powerless to collect taxes from companies based on their turf.

All that was required was for one or two States not to levy additional gaming taxes. So off the big companies trotted - Coral, Stan James and Ladbrokes to tax-friendly Gibraltar, and William Hill to Antigua. Sitting by your computer in Torquay, Barcelona or even Kuala Lumpur, it made no difference where the bookie was technically 'based'. The deal was pretty good all round. The bookies could, in theory, enjoy much higher turnover as a result of offering 'no tax' betting to punters who had previously been constrained by their national governments. Also they were in a position to take bets from countries where gambling was discouraged altogether.

The companies have experienced mixed results. Stan James and Victor Chandler have had no qualms about accepting huge football bets from clients in the Far East, even those attempting massive arbitrages with prices offered locally. Coral/Eurobet, however, reported substantial losses from their website operation, partially down to the fact that in the first major tournament they accepted Far East bets - Euro 2000 - there was a dull procession of favoured teams winning, most of whom had been supported by Oriental high rollers.

This, incidentally, has a pleasant implication for most of the betting tactics that I will explore. As I am firmly on the side of ignoring dull favoured teams and looking for less obvious results, anyone following my broad tactical advice is really doing their bookie quite a favour. Even if we get well ahead long-term, we are effectively helping our bookmaker to make a balanced book.

The situation from October 2001 is that there are no longer any tax additions to stake money for betting on the Net, the phone, or now and most radically, in your high street. This levelling of the playing field should have some interesting consequences for the relative popularity of the three ways of betting in the UK. The internet, while on the surface, quick, convenient and cheap, has its frustrations. We demand perfection, in terms of site design, fast loading pages and transparency of rules.

Despite the time taken to get there, high street shops are a comparatively risk-free environment for punters. When the cashier hands you the carbon copy of your slip you know that the bet is on. Online, the experience of clicking a mouse button to confirm a bet and then getting an error message, signalling that you have to start again, is painfully frustrating. Worse still is a message that doesn't make it clear whether you have placed the bet or not.

Some sites suffer major design problems - the most irritating of which is to force you to load a complete page in order to get access to just a set of odds for a single match. If all the talk of 'band-width' improvements and faster access comes to pass, the situation should improve quickly - but, in the meantime, I'm sure I'm not unique in being prone to internet rage.

Wherever you bet, the importance of tax-free punting can easily be overlooked. Bearing in mind my previous comments about the consequences of moving into the 100 per cent performance bracket, think back to what it was like when nine per cent of your stake had to be added in duty. A £100 bet, tax paid, actually cost £109. You probably faced between a 5-10 per cent margin built into the odds (depending whether or not you were taking the best prices on offer). This margin meant that, in effect, you were only returned £90-95 for every £100 staked. Purely to beat the odds you had to make up the 5-10 per cent to haul you over the £100 mark again - a difficult but not impossible task. But the imposition of tax meant you had to win back another nine per cent simply to break even (achieve a betting performance of 100 per cent).

This caught many punters in a hopeless grey area of marginal losses. They were good enough to beat the odds but were not quite good enough to beat the odds *and* tax on top. So they were mercilessly caught in the performance bracket just short of 100 per cent - i.e. making them long-term losers. But as the tax has been swept away they are suddenly, miraculously sitting in 100 per cent plus territory, even though their skill remains the same.

In yesteryear, they had to pay tax and were basically doomed long-term; today they can shovel on stakes in the expectation of getting ahead. The implications for this are superb for football punters. In many areas of football betting there are marginal opportunities, where betting on a certain pattern of results manages to beat the overall odds long-term, albeit by not much.

One of the longest running football betting loopholes is the fact that Hills handicap list (where the away team is given a goal head start) is priced in such a way as to make it possible to enjoy perhaps a five per cent profit long-term by sticking to away win forecasts. This bet is available in Hills shops but not on their website. Paying tax, I found it was barely possible to get ahead long-term by betting in trebles - we are talking an overall profit of a fraction of a percent, not really worth doggedly pursuing. But with no tax, the game can only have one winner. The profit margin in the punter's favour is now over 10 times what it was.

Tax was, in many respects, a useful buffer that prevented big staking gamblers from taking bookies to the cleaners. The major firms are publicly rubbing their hands with glee at the prospect of increasing their turnover - but you have to ask, what sort of turnover are they expecting? The sadly and chronically addicted losing gamblers don't have any more pennies to contribute - the lack of tax simply makes their money go a bit further. A certain amount of new profitable business (for the bookie) will be generated, but a vast slice of the new turnover cake will be added by a smallish band of winning, or borderline winning, clients. They, as we have seen, will suddenly stake vastly more than previously in order to turn their small profit margins into hard cash.

The chairman of Hills, John Brown, has addressed the issue by stating that the modern day firms will have to be prepared to become more like the bookies of the old days - prepared to take substantial risks and accept that they can't just expect to sit back and expect to chisel away the same margins as before. The betting industry has previously been seen to act in a somewhat monopolistic way. Whenever one company raised its margins on football betting, the rest gleefully followed. At the beginning of the 2000-01 season, industry spokesmen suggested that the gradual rise in margins we have seen in the last 20 years would not be sustained. The degree of genuine competition in the market should ensure that this is the case.

From a punter's point of view, there has never been a better time to get into football betting. If we can't manage to win in the highly liberalised betting environment of the first decade of this century, then we'll never be able to.

chapter **three**

# who, why and where?

Asking 'who is the best bookie?' across the different types of betting now available begs the question, 'best for whom?' As far as we are concerned the more disorganised, inexperienced and poorly controlled a firm, the better it must be for us. It needn't be quite as clear cut as this, but different firms do have characteristics that suit different styles of betting. Many people who hold a variety of different accounts will report the strange phenomena of consistently being able to beat one firm but always lose to another.

There is a widely held belief amongst the not-so-serious betting shop fraternity that William Hill offer better prices on football. There has been some tinkering with the over-rounds recently which meant that at various times one company could legitimately be said to be more attractive. But at the time I first examined this, back in the early 90s, all the major companies bet to the same over-round of 111 per cent. The only possible reason why this perception exists is that Hills stick their neck out more with their football prices - i.e. although they bet to the same over-round, they are slightly more likely than by chance to be offering a better price on an individual team.

I have always had the distinct impression that Hills name crops up more than other bookmaker when it comes to strange, out-of-line, or plain incorrect prices. On the other hand, Britain's other big player, Ladbrokes, has a well deserved reputation as being solidly unbeatable. Apart from a couple of occasions where their prices had gone awry (recounted later on), I have always found them difficult to beat to the extent that I rarely pay them a visit. Their profits have ensured that Ladbrokes newer branches are the smartest shops of all the high street firms.

Around 50 per cent of my fixed-odds turnover is with Hills - which considering the large number of other firms, gives some indication of my estimation of their 'beatability'. Of the other major UK firms, Coral are reasonably solid on day-to-day prices but sometimes look vulnerable on their special bets.

I found it remarkably easy to give Stanley Racing some punishment when they mucked up some prices on the number of goals in Premiership matches; and I suspect the Tote, whose outlets always seem to be hidden away where you least expect them, might still be very shaky with similar prices.

Of all the bookmakers to go on a limb and offer prices on a variety of new markets, Stan James are the kings of the jungle. They were the first firm to offer fixed-odds bets updated in-running (bravely) and their specials on the number of bookings, corners and time of the first goal are a decent attempt at muscling in on spread betting territory. Their website is super-fast loading and well designed. I would hesitate to call them 'easy to beat' but the fact that they have invented many markets means that many of their odds cannot be compared to their competitors.

Where there is no benchmark for prices a company can be at its most vulnerable. As a general principle, this is always worth looking out for. When a company offers precisely the same market as another, it is relatively easy to compare prices and only have a wager at the best that is on offer. The benefit is good up to a point, but where a company prices a speciality market blind (where they are the only firm offering odds), errors can frequently creep in.

We have become conditioned to accept that the words 'exciting' and 'fast-growing' naturally occur whenever spread betting is mentioned. The first is certainly true, but the second would be more than a slight overstatement. Ladbrokes' Sporting Spreads was launched in such an upbeat way as to suggest spread betting was about to eclipse their involvement in traditional fixed-odds. Fifteen years on, having seen Ladbrokes and Hills scuttle out of spread betting, it is the old style fixed-odds that are still dominating the sports betting scene.

Sporting Index have done an extraordinary job in consistently hanging on to around 50 per cent of the spread betting market share. They propelled the whole concept skyward with their own brand of quirky humour, excellent customer care and bold marketing. They are also incredibly difficult to beat.

Almost slipping through the back door, they introduced performance spreads on each individual team in all the English divisions. This was effectively the first time that British punters could bet on a single league game without having to find other selections to satisfy the rules on the minimum amount of forecasts we could have in a line.

The hated 'five-folds only' has thankfully bitten the dust but we are still left with being required to place a minimum of trebles on most British league games. This betting rule was introduced by the Football League (who awkwardly own the copyright to football fixtures) following match-fixing revelations in the early 60s.

In many respects the rule helped bookmakers. By imposing restrictions on the minimum number of selections that could be included in a line, the bookmakers encouraged the culture of seeing football betting as mildly diverting lottery-type game, where the punter took pot luck with a hastily assembled 10-fold. It was probably thanks to Sporting Index that a process has started that should see the official abolition of the 'no-singles' rule. Surrey and Bet Direct now offer singles on Premiership matches (with Ladbrokes planning to go the same way) and some offshore internet firms are quietly offering singles on all league matches.

There are probably close to 30,000 individuals who regularly spread bet in Britain. But, for the time being, the talk is more of consolidating rather than expanding the industry. Fundamentally, spread betting fails to have much addictive quality, which is probably best for the well-being of the nation. But the result is that the spread companies have to battle against a small number of clued-up clients without the vast army of consistently losing punters who contribute to the coffers of the fixed-odds firms.

There is an almost unnoticed pattern of small but frequent losses that are the bread and butter of the traditional bookies' business. In the punter's mind losses are quickly discounted in favour of magnifying the importance of wins. Over a series of bets the punter can be lulled into a sense that they are up or at least around level, long-term.

Fixed-odds punters may have ghastly losing runs, but they rarely face a crisis of confidence that makes them give up betting altogether. The fixed-odds bookie, meanwhile, is equally satisfied to know that his client is contributing a healthy margin without really knowing it. And that is how the whole crazy industry survives.

Yet spread betting shares none of these important attributes. There is a spectre of a large loss that hangs over account holders and, by implication, the spread firms. One in 25 trades might result in hitting the wrong end of a stop-loss, enough to turn an enthusiastic account holder scurrying back to the relative safety of fixed-odds punting.

Big losses, paradoxically, don't help the firms either as they can signal the end of an account. Spread firms are unnaturally in the position of needing punters to lose steadily over time while avoiding the hand-wringing that results from a spectacular loss.

The hottest betting innovation in the UK at present is the person-to-person website, characterised by Betfair. At a time when so many companies espoused the future of the internet without really knowing why, the person-to-person sites use the web to its fullest potential. Here punters offer prices to other punters within the framework of the operating company who take a small cut from each wager.

Though in its relative infancy, this strand of betting has taken off spectacularly. Already there are individuals who are willing to price up every single runner in a horse race, shaving a point or two off each runner's price. As bookies' football prices generally contain a smaller margin than horse races, there is only limited scope for offering better odds.

The operations of the betting exchanges will ensure that traditional companies will not be allowed the freedom to raise margins substantially in the future, as the free market of the exchanges will become too attractive to online punters. The concept has now been extended to spread betting with the launch of Intrade - essentially a sports betting broker along the lines of the operation of financial markets.

The one difficulty the new exchanges may face is that each company is reliant upon a strong pool of account holders to ensure plenty of two-way action. From everyone's point of view it would actually probably be best if there was just one vast global betting exchange, as long as it was well run. The launch of new companies could dissolve the base of the established ones, leading to an unfortunate situation where the whole sector strangles itself through competition.

For the time being, the appetite for internet start-ups is weak and we have to hope that the innovators in this field can be left to get on with it. Person-to-person betting, where the bookie disappears altogether, uses the potential of the internet in a particularly ingenious way. Betting has almost come full circle. The rise of the multi-national bookmaking organisation appears to be giving away to a model that is based more on the legacy of casual betting between two people in a pub - albeit aided by advanced technology.

chapter **four**

# fractional odds and other vices

The internet has ensured that English is steadily becoming the world's most spoken language, but otherwise the rest of the planet is less keen to embrace some of our exports. The British bookmaking industry is rightly considered as very strong internationally, but the continentals have more or less given up on our quaint way of describing bookmakers' prices - fractional odds.

Fractional odds are a ghost from pre-decimalisation, which is why they don't even have a passing similarity to the base 10 monetary system that we've had in Britain for over 30 years. Hence a price of 8-11 pays you a cumbersome £17.27p (and even then the pennies have to be rounded).

Continental bookmakers now exclusively use the 'dividend' system, where the price tells you how much you will paid for a correct selection. So '2.20' gives a return of 2.20 multiplied by your stake. It is likely that the bookies with an international client base will have to try to force the Brits into line. At present they tend to set prices using fractional odds and then convert them to the dividend system, but this simply means that punters in Holland and elsewhere are left scratching their heads at dividend prices of 2.88 (15-8).

I don't intend to present a beginner's guide to odds, but there are some points worth bearing in mind that can confuse the most experienced punters. Any set of odds in Britain can now be described in three ways - the fractional odds (6-4), the dividend (2.50) and a percentage (40 per cent). I tend to think as the dividend as the odds plus one - i.e. six divided by four equals 1.5 - plus one = 2.5. The percentage is found by dividing the dividend into 100 - i.e. 100 divided by 2.5 = 40 per cent. Others might have totally different ways of getting to the same answer.

Each of these types of ways of describing the odds can be employed at different times. Most British football punters still tend to visualise games in terms of fractional odds. A 7-2 shot playing away from home is a touch worse than the average away team's chances. However, if initially presented with the dividend odds of 4.50, many of us have to do a bit of a mental double-take to convert it back to 7-2, before fully comprehending the information.

Percentages are perhaps the best way to imagine odds and the associated chance of 'something' actually happening. All the odds and dividends can be arranged along a scale from 0 per cent (where there is absolutely no chance) to 100 per cent (mathematical certainty. Absolute 0 per cent can't actually be expressed in terms of fractional odds, as the scale is infinite.

Thinking in terms of percentages helps smooth out the misconceptions of fractional odds. If a team suddenly sinks from 50-1 to 25-1 to win their division, it may look as though they have become world-beaters, when in fact their estimated chance of success has gone from 1.96 per cent to 3.85 per cent - a rather more modest looking blip.

In theory each set of odds is an estimate of an event happening. But for bookies to make a theoretical profit on each event, we know they have to build a profit margin into the odds. I will assume the reader has a reasonable understanding of the 'over-round' built into the overall odds for one match or event, but the way in which this over-round effects a single price may need clarifying.

When we see a price of 6-4 for Chesterfield to win a match, the odds reflect the bookie's estimate of the true chances of them winning, minus a margin. If their opponents are also 6-4 to win, and the draw is priced at 11-5, the total of all the percentages is 111.25. In theory the bookie only has to pay out £100 for every £111.25p he takes in stakes. His profit margin looks as though it is 11.25 per cent - in fact it's a slightly less 10.1 per cent (11.25 as a percentage of 111.25). So we must assume that each of the three prices has a margin of 10 per cent built in.

Chesterfield's price of 6-4 equals a percentage of 40 per cent, but the bookmaker has already added a margin into the price on offer. To get back to his 'true' estimate of the chances of them winning, we must knock 10 per cent off the 40 per cent that is implied in the odds.

In this case knocking 10 per cent off 40 per cent looks like it would come to 30 per cent. Here lies the important difference between percentages and percentage points. Which calculation applies depends on the situation. It is common to hear phrases like, "Conservative Party support has dropped from 32 per cent last month to 28 per cent this month - a dip of four points." But in

Chesterfield's case we are looking for the true percentage drop; 10 per cent of 40 is four. Subtracting four from 40 equals 36.

We can therefore say that the odds compilers' true estimate of a Chesterfield win is 36 per cent - so 'fair' odds should probably be 7-4, rather than 6-4. This 'knocking off the margin' calculation is fairly central to a lot of football betting principles. Say we wanted to find out the true chance of landing a treble on Birmingham, Tranmere and Oldham, where the odds on each of our teams are 4-6.

Firstly, take Birmingham's chances: 4-6 equals a chance of 60 per cent, but we will assume there is a 10 per cent margin built in, so their true chance is only 54 per cent. Tranmere also have the same 54 per cent chance. So the chance of both winning is 54 per cent of 54 per cent (29 per cent). Next up is Oldham, bringing their 54 per cent chance into the equation. The 29 per cent of the first two winning is cut down to 15.75 per cent (54 per cent of 29). The slightly-less-than 16 per cent chance we are left with as an estimate of the true chance of landing the treble may be intuitively somewhat meagre compared to what we might have expected.

But the true horror of this bet is fully revealed when we go expectantly to the payout counter. The treble pays £4.66 for every £1 of stake, just over 7-2 overall. The bookie is actually paying you as if the treble had a 21.5 per cent chance of being successful. However, we already know that the true chances were around 16 per cent. The payout for a 16 per cent chance should have been £6.35; instead we got a measly £4.66. We effectively lost £1.69 for every pound staked, or over 26 per cent of what we should have won had the odds been fair.

The margin of 10 per cent in the bookie's favour, had we bet on any of the three games in singles, has suddenly mushroomed to 26 per cent when we place a treble. Here we can see how a margin in the bookie's favour can multiply through a bet horrendously. At this point you might be expecting me to implore you only ever to bet in singles. In fact, personally I very rarely bet with combinations less than trebles.

Profit margins can work both ways. If the bookie has a 10 per cent margin on each single leg of a multiple bet, then the theoretical margin in their favour gets larger every time you add another leg. So their margin is bigger if you bet trebles rather than singles, and is larger still if you bet five-folds.

But exactly the same principle works in reverse. It was only comparatively recently that I realised I'd been using multiple bets too meekly. If you are sure you have a five per cent margin on each of 10 bets, then you should ramp up the multiples. The more the certainty, the more multiple bets you should have in bigger combinations.

It might seem a somewhat hair-raising proposition, but the proof of this comes with a 'time-machine' scenario. Having perfected the art of time travel, you set the dials to the morning of a Saturday last month, armed with a copy of the Sunday papers listing the football results for the previous day. Considering you know what the results are already, how do you maximise your profits?

There is clearly not a lot to be gained messing around with singles, doubles, etc. All you need is £1 on a massive 20-fold and you'll effortlessly break through the bookie's payout limit. Theoretically, the bigger your advantage is, the bigger the multiple bet should be.

Back in the real world, there are a few more nuts and bolts of margins that need consideration. You may be aware of the extraordinary £500,000 win in 2001 by Mick Gibbs, a 59-year-old roofer from Lichfield, who managed to predict the winners of just about all the British divisions and various cup competitions. I wouldn't want to diminish this incredible betting feat, but I do rather suspect we have heard this story a number of times before in previous seasons. There does seem to be a familiar pattern, where one of the big firms reveals a staggeringly huge win by a punter for small stakes, using exactly the same technique of lining up loads of divisional winners.

There is perhaps a good reason for bookies to be so pleased to tell about their misfortune - and it comes back to the subject of margins. Each division has up to 24 teams. The greater the possible number winners, the higher the margins built in (though there is no particularly logical reason why this should be the case). The big firms want us to place bets on high margin markets; so to make us believe that we too can scoop the jackpot, they like to publicise big winners on markets where the margins are at their highest.

As a general rule, I immediately rule out any type of bet where there are more than four possible results. Just as in horse racing, the fewer the number of runners, the smaller the margins built into the odds. If you want to have a bet on Rochdale to do well in their division, then you should really be buying them on a spread firm's 'total season's points' market, or backing them in a match bet to finish higher than a single other team.

In cases like this, where there are only two possible results, bookies will tend to bet to 106 per cent, superior to betting on the 'three-result' games themselves, and vastly better than correct score bets or backing teams to win their divisions. Most bookmakers price individual matches to 112. This has crept up a couple of points in the last 10 years, though there are clear reasons why. In 1990, there were only five major firms independently offering odds, plus a handful of small operators. At the last count, there were 84 bookmakers who could be accessed through a British computer and who were offering odds on English Premiership games - though, realistically, punters will have more faith in names they are familiar with. As things stand, there are so many companies out there that if it were possible to take the best prices offered on the three possible results of a football match, you could whittle down the theoretical margin in favour of the bookies until it evaporates completely.

The fact that it is frequently possible to bet with different companies on the same game to ensure a profit, prompted the launch of a number of internet sites dedicated to collating vast reams of odds from the worlds different bookmakers. But the pooling of this information is as much use to the bookmakers as it is punters, seeing as the firms listed can, like everyone else, check whether their prices are out of line.

On the issue of differential pricing between firms, we are slightly in danger of arriving back at the point where we all started. Instead of having a small number of companies offering bets at low margins, we are liable to end up with a vast number of firms betting to huge theoretical margins in order to protect themselves.

Even if bookmakers are able to access information about their competitors' match odds, there is nobody collating the prices on the huge variety of speciality bets. In such markets, whether it be on the number of goals scored in a game or which manager will get the sack during the season, price differences can float around endlessly without being spotted. For this reason alone, it's worth keeping an eagle-eye on the more esoteric markets.

## 32 . successful football betting

chapter five

# forecasting pitfalls

Before going on to look at some of the factors that are genuinely useful in football betting, I thought I'd have a go at slaying a few sacred cows on the subject - the misconceptions that can easily crop up and ruin and otherwise good strategy.

The popularity of football around the globe is frequently attributed to a number of frankly misty-eyed reasons. These are based on tribal loyalties, an escape from poverty, the artistry of the game, etc. In fact, football has had a large slice of good fortune in its development that has helped propel it onwards and upwards. Underlying its basic popularity is one of the main reasons as to why trying to predict the result of a football match can be so frustrating.

Uniquely amongst sports, not a great deal happens in a game during 90 minutes play. In top class football there are fewer than three goals in each game. In terms of time on the field of play divided by the number of scoring opportunities, football appears to rank very low in terms of the frequency of decisive scoring moments.

Compare this to basketball, where there is a score every half-minute or so - or golf, where a hole is completed in close to half the time that football fans need to wait for a goal to appear. But clearly there is something attractive about the fact that goals are relatively few and far between. Each one is met with a sudden emotional outpouring, from both players and spectators.

It was significant that when FIFA tentatively suggested that the size of the goals be increased (following the goal drought of the World Cup in 1990) there were howls of outrage from all parts of the football community. From an impartial viewpoint FIFA had a case. The size of the goals remains unchanged from Victorian times, when the physical stature of humans in general, and goalkeepers in particular, was tiny compared to what it is today. Basically it was much easier to score, especially by lobbing the comparatively tiny goalies.

As we all stopped eating gruel and started knocking back the added vitamins and hormones in modern food, we grew larger throughout the 20th century. In combination with the grip of defensive tactics, the goal count went down. On a day in 1969 the most frequent scoreline in British football critically changed from 2-1 to 1-1. The current number of goals per game is important in establishing the balance between teams. As it stands now, the naturally better team usually wins, but finds it quite a task to do so. The number of 'shock' results is satisfyingly high so as not to make a match a foregone conclusion.

You might be tempted to say that this is the case with most sports, but the way in which games are scored plays a vital role in determining how easy it is for a better person or team to win. Tennis, for example, has a peculiar, albeit successful, scoring mechanism in terms of letting the better player win. Anyone who plays the game regularly, particularly if they play against one other partner most of the time, will perhaps recognise tennis's strange characteristic of ensuring that it only takes one player to be marginally better than their opponent to ensure victory on almost every single occasion.

The opposite is true of golf, where the way in which the game is scored tends to lead to a disproportionate number of freak results. Because of the large number of chance factors in determining the winner, it should be difficult for a single player to dominate the game for a long period of their career, as is the case in tennis. This makes the all-conquering achievements of Tiger Woods seem all the more extraordinary.

Imagine if the size of football goals was suddenly increased to about 25-foot wide by 15-foot. To score, one team would simply need to keep possession of the ball until they reached the vicinity of the opponent's penalty-area and then shoot from long-range. In such a scenario a slight difference in the team's abilities would be amply reflected in the result, which might be a win by 19-4. There would almost never be draws or shock results. It is inconceivable that a non-league team could ever come close to beating a Premiership side.

As football stands it is almost perfectly set up for an exciting contest, even if there are quite marked differences in natural ability. A team can spend millions on the finest players in the world but still only manage to scrape through against an altogether more impoverished club. But scrape through they usually do - it is equally important that the balance between sides does not disintegrate into a total lottery, where chance factors alone determine the result. The essential appeal of the game, therefore, is that it's actually quite difficult to forecast the result. If we were fairly sure who would win in advance, football's appeal would largely be lost. It is against this uncertain background that we have to pick our bets.

But there is another characteristic of football that is almost unique in top-flight sport that provides the main hurdle to forecasting results. With football the question of *who* is playing is dwarfed by the consideration of *where* they are playing. The bare facts are that a professional team playing at their home ground is almost twice as likely to win as a team playing away from home.

The natural home advantage of football teams is not really mirrored elsewhere in international sport. Even when a Test cricket team has to live in another country for months on end in order to play a series (often in a distinctly different environment to their own), they do not suffer the dramatic loss of form of a football team that travels a couple of hours up a British motorway.

In fact much of football betting is focussed on trying to determine what factors contribute to home advantage and finding the times at which it doesn't apply. In order to illustrate how home advantage swamps the actual abilities of players, imagine a game between two clubs of roughly equal ability who play each other at a neutral venue. For the sake of argument, we'll say that Newcastle United and West Ham are evenly matched sides.

If they were to play at Villa Park, a bookie may offer prices of 6-4 for both teams, with the draw at 11-5. However, if the venue was to be mysteriously switched to St James' Park, a fair set of odds might be Newcastle 5-6, West Ham 11-4, the draw 9-4. These prices roughly reflect the sudden implied superiority of Newcastle at home.

If it were suddenly within the power of West Ham to address the perceived advantage of Newcastle and act to redress the balance, what could they do? The directors at Upton Park get their heads together and decide that the only way to get back on an even keel is to go on a spending spree. By a strange coincidence, that very day, the entire Brazilian national squad becomes available on the transfer market for the modest price of £200m. The chequebook comes out and on a wet Wednesday night on Tyneside, the Brazilians turn out in West Ham's colours. What effect has this had on their odds of beating Newcastle?

My guess is that West Ham might have managed to claw their way back to a rating of 6-4, exactly the same as how they would have started had the game been played at a neutral venue. In effect, the difference in the relative fortunes of home and away teams completely engulfs the natural abilities of the two teams.

The slightly mysterious dominance of home teams colours every aspect of football betting. To take this into account, it is useful to see any individual football match as being subject to a home/away 'template' based on the relative fortunes of the hosts and visitors in a particular competition or league. If two Premiership sides meet, their contest must be seen against the background of all Premier League games. In a large sample of such games it becomes clear that about 48 per cent of games are home wins, 27 per cent are drawn and 25 per cent are away wins.

The odds on two teams who are equally rated in terms of ability, league standing, etc must be based around these core home/away frequencies. If the home team is deemed slightly superior overall, then their odds must reflect this, moving to an equivalent of, say, a 53 per cent chance of victory. If the away team is naturally better than their implied chance of victory, then they must move up above the usual 25 per cent mark. The slightly irritating aspect of this is that the imbalance of home/away results ensures that hosts, who by any rational analysis are 'worse' than the visitors, manage to start favourites to win the game.

## who's going to win - and does it matter?

The home/away conundrum leads to all sorts of initial difficulties with forecasting. The lists of '1-X-2' predictions published in most of the daily papers are a throwback to the days when the pools were the most popular form of football betting. Here the paper's tipster assigns each match a predicted result. A brief look at the pattern of forecasts reveals one of the basic pitfalls of predicting results. You will find that around 60 per cent of all forecasts are for home wins, with perhaps 20 per cent marked as draws and the other 20 per cent away wins.

Homes are vastly over-represented, as we know that less than 50 per cent of games actually result in a home win. Correspondingly, aways and draws are under-predicted. It is not difficult to see why. The chances of a draw in an individual match hardly deviate from around 27 per cent. On the first coupon that I happen to have to hand, in only three of the 66 matches listed is the away team the favourite. This means that in the other 63 games the home side is rated at least as likely to win as the visitors.

So if you want to predict who is going to win a British football game, you might as well always plump for the home side, except in a tiny minority of matches. That way you are more or less guaranteed to achieve at least a 45 per cent success rate. This is basically what the tipsters do - simply shove a disproportionate number of games down as home wins. The more away wins and draws they include, over time, the worst their ability to find the correct result.

This leads inevitably to an unsettling conclusion - that in some ways it is relatively easy to predict the result of a football game. For the vast majority of matches the answer must be 'home win'. So here it is important to distinguish the difference between forecasting the result and finding which team to bet on. It is remarkable that there is sometimes confusion over this issue. Certain high-profile ex-managers and commentators give tips on the major firm's shops TV coverage. For a game like Arsenal v Middlesbrough, we are earnestly told that Arsenal might be "a little to strong" for Boro'. This seems rather blindingly obvious.

There is a world of difference between stating that Arsenal are favourites and trying to assess the correct odds. Should they be as short as 4-11 or as long as 8-15? This is the only task in hand - assessing whether the odds are correct in relation to the true chance of each result occurring. It's why many so-called forecasting techniques, which do not relate results to the odds on offer, are of little value, despite their apparently highly technical nature.

The essential problem with traditional forecasting (based on all the known information about two teams) relates back to the point of football being inherently exciting because of its unpredictability. We sometimes tend to assume that football matches must possess a quality that allows us, with a degree of endeavour, to predict the result correctly - it just seems like a matter of using the right information. A brief look at any team's recent results tends to demonstrate that this might be over-optimistic.

In fact, the recent form of most teams is an eccentric hotch-potch of results - a couple of expected wins, mixed with an odd looking draw, a heavy away defeat and an unexpected away win. Over the course of the whole season, the best tend to rise to the top of their divisions, but their individual results demonstrate an almost meaningless 'two steps back, one step forward' type of pattern. Academics in the 1980's suggested that the results of football games barely reflected the difference in abilities of the teams.

None of this has prevented concerted efforts to design computer-based prediction systems. A groundbreaking work in this respect was Drapkin and Forsyth's 1987 book, *The Punters Revenge*. Previous published attempts to suggest a comprehensive football prediction system were thin on the ground. Highly influential, the book has spawned a whole culture of football betting systems. The authors searched for a way to take all known relevant form information in to account. The assessment of a team's current strength was based on how they performed against previous opponents, using the strength ratings of these teams at the time of the match. The system therefore provided a much more accurate assessment of the relative strengths of teams than any analysis of league tables.

Indeed, as a forecasting model, Paul Steele, in *The Football Betting Guide*, demonstrated that it was vastly superior to any other system in terms of predicting raw results. But there doesn't appear to be any published data as to how the Power Ratings model performs in terms of beating the odds on offer. Does use of the system really produce a performance of over 100 per cent? I confess I haven't tested it myself but my suspicion is that it falls slightly short. The problem with virtually all forecasting models is that they fall into the same trap - that of the 'singing from the same hymn sheet' phenomena.

For example, you try to forecast the result of a game in which Liverpool are at home to Sunderland. The odds for a Liverpool win are 2-5. We know that such games are not always the forgone conclusions they look on paper. But what the odds suggest, and what any analysis must surely point to, is a home win. In fact there is at least a 35 per cent chance that Liverpool will *not* win the game, but there is unlikely to be anything lurking in the available information that would pick this out. There is only a very small minority of games, perhaps 10 per cent, where it really is impossible to pick a favourite.

What invariably happens is that any detailed computer-aided analysis tends to throw back answers that we could have guessed in around 10 seconds by a cursory look at a league table. Humans (odds compilers amongst them), and computers that are programmed by humans, will rarely disagree about forecasts. What the computer sees is a relatively tranquil scene in which better teams tend to beat their opponents, and teams that are close in standard will probably draw. They are actually 'thinking' in the same way as the odds compilers. What we really want is a bit of software that can tell us when the runaway league leaders are going to be held to a 0 - 0 draw by a bunch of no-hopers. By feeding in the known information about previous results it is very unlikely that any forecasting model can pick out these sorts of oddities.

In general, I tend to stick to the philosophy that the main thrust of football betting endeavours should be aimed at trying to predict when the more unexpected results are going to happen. This doesn't necessarily meaning constantly backing a string of long-shots, but it does mean that my favoured strategy is to try to pick the occasions where the 'obvious' is not going to happen. This effectively means putting oneself in a position opposed to any answer that a rational look at previous results might indicate. The key in all betting is to back results that are underestimated in the odds. To do this properly you have to bury into the detail of two teams significantly more than that of the compilers to find a factor that has not been taken in to account in the odds.

The question of which information has been assimilated into the odds is vital. Information that has already been taken into account is basically useless. Consider two different reasons to back Millwall at 1-2 in a fictitious Saturday home game with Rotherham. Firstly, "Millwall have won their last three home games on the trot, scoring eight goals. They should be too strong for the lacklustre South Yorkshire outfit." Secondly, "Rotherham come into the game following the mysterious dropping of their captain for their midweek game. A dressing-room dispute over wages is clearly behind this, and seven players have requested transfer listings."

There is a vast difference between the assimilation rating of the two bits of information. The first tells us nothing that even the most hungover odds compiler could have missed. The raw information on current form is, along with the league standing, the basis of the odds. Any betting advice on these grounds is playing straight into the bookmakers' hands. They know the current record of Millwall; you (and everybody else) know precisely the same thing. There are no grounds for betting.

The same is not true of the 'dressing-room bust-up' scenario. Since the odds were set the previous Monday, it can't possibly be taken into account. In this situation you might assume there was a factor significantly in Millwall's favour that wasn't reflected in their quote of 1-2. This is a fairly clear cut case of there being firm evidence that Millwall may be slightly undervalued in their odds.

The above, deliberately over-exaggerated example, is clearly a piece of breaking news, the type of which is comparatively rare in football circles. However, there are certainly opportunities to benefit from raw statistical information that is being ignored in the framing of the odds. Somewhere between the two extremes of the above examples lies a magical threshold - the point at which information is, and is not, taken in to account. To one side the information is useless, to the other is the stuff we really want to discover.

It is certainly possible that some fairly basic information about current form and league position may just about lie on 'our' side of the line. Further on, I explore some techniques involving the analysis of this. The most marginal opportunities lie in the field of whether a team's current form is out of kilter with its league position. Occasionally, I suspect, such fairly basic information is enough to get a slight advantage, but it's lies at the dodgy end of the spectrum of factors that may get us ahead long-term. The most powerful techniques tend to use statistics in a way that most other punters would never dream of.

Overall, the way that the majority of football fans go about forecasting and betting on the results of matches is very much in our favour. There is a marked tendency to see the game in a strangely concrete way. Despite the clear evidence that football is a highly unpredictable game, followers, many with vastly much more knowledge of its intricacies than me, still express astonishment that odd results ever happen at all. This is particularly true of opinions towards the England team, some of which add up to an inexplicable national malaise. In the few days leading up to an England international, you'll hardly find a soul who offer anything less than a 3-0 victory as a forecast (though this may be tempered to 1-0 if we're up against someone really hard, like France).

After the obligatory 0-0 draw, the public throws all the toys out of its collective pram, murmurs start about the managers parentage and we have to endure pundits moaning about the crisis in our game. But come the following month, whether changes have been made or not, everyone starts playing the old CD again, going back to the usual optimistic predictions of a victory at a canter.

## strong favourites - a case of blind faith?

I must confess that the first football bet I ever placed was a five-fold on one of the strongest favourites in each of five divisions. I suppose I was caught by the promise of 'Guaranteed odds of 9-1' for five homes emblazoned on the heading of the football coupon. The fact that virtually all the bookmakers persist in using this type of banner suggests that it performs some sort of profitable function for them.

Five apparent dead certainties at 1-2 multiplies together to produce a return of £75.94p to a £10 stake. This looks reasonably achievable. But in fact it is an illusion based on our general inability to be instinctively able to make correct estimates when multiplying numbers together.

It happens to all us of, from maths professors to the most numerically challenged. Even a fairly innocuous sum of 1 x 2 x 3 x 4 x 5, if you merely glance at it, looks as though it should result in not a lot more than 40, whereas people genuinely express surprise at finding the answer is really 120. The result is that when you try to guess how much you're five-fold at skinny odds will return, the accumulative odds on offer actually look rather enticing.

Most football bettors suffer from a similar type of 'favourititis'. It would appear that those staking £20,000 per game in the Far East are just as prone to this malady as the betting shop fraternity with their 20p eight-folds. If we could compile a huge list of every price of every team that featured in football bets the previous year, we might find the average price at which a team was backed was something near 4-7. As a species we are hooked on football favourites.

In 1994, and again in 1997, I attempted to find out whether there was anything inherently wrong with consistently backing the favourites. It was clear that a huge number of people lined up the five, six or more shortest-priced teams on the coupon. Since so little money was attracted to the outsiders or the draw, the odds compilers might be tempted to constrict the prices even more on strong favourites as they would probably see no loss of turnover, but increased profits. On both occasions I found that you were naturally better off avoiding very short-priced teams. Performance backing the 'certainties' was around six per cent less than if you always stuck with outsiders.

Just to demonstrate that football betting statistics are a moving target, I was amazed to learn from Derek McGovern's book, *Sports Gambling... And How To Make It Pay* that, in 1999, many of the short-priced teams, notably Manchester United, had become undervalued in the odds, with nasty consequences for firms as they ploughed through the mass of coupons that featured United, Celtic, etc in multiple bets. In other words the widening advantage of the top sides had not been spotted by the bookies. In all the home games of the sides who finished in the top four (76 matches) there were only four defeats. In terms of odds this meant that the average away odds for sides in these matches should have been priced in the region of a staggering 16-1 - unheard of in British football.

In 2001, I returned to the subject and again ploughed through the stats on the performance of strong favourites. Grudgingly, at the time of writing, it would appear that so-called banker games do appear to be living up to their reputation, though I can't see the situation lasting very long.

In 2000-2001 the top Premiership clubs of Manchester United, Arsenal, Liverpool and Chelsea (teams who when playing at home tend to feature on a vastly disproportionate number of coupons) all would have produced a profit had you backed them to level stakes in all of their 19 games. In fact there was a profit of 20 per cent in backing all teams rated at under 1-2 to win their home games throughout the Premiership in this season. Over all four of the English Divisions, had you backed every single home team in 2000-2001, you would have retained 92 per cent of your total stake. Backing draws retained 88 per cent of stakes, while away wins only returned 81 per cent of stake money. This seems to demonstrate that home teams are, at present, consistently undervalued in the betting. This could be something of a timebomb for the bookies as they are offering over-generous odds on exactly the sort of teams that most punters want to back. If this continues into this tax-free era the traditional firms are facing getting stung badly by those occasional punters from whom they should be taking the most profits long-term.

They are also leaving themselves open to anyone placing large wagers on very short-priced teams (a habit that deductions largely wiped out as the proportion of tax to the potential win was simply too large to make the tactic worthwhile). Keep a close eye on any wholesale adjustment to prices on strong home favourites. My guess is that the major firms will have to start discouraging 'banker' wagers by constricting very short prices even further. There is a good argument for slapping on prices of 1-8 and lower on teams like Manchester United at home. If this eventually happens, then some much needed value by going against the obvious way will reappear.

## ringing the changes

The example of the apparent upturn in fortunes of the strongest sides illustrates the ever-changing face of football stats. This can happen by changes in the laws of the game, different tactical considerations or a host of other factors. A key betting opportunity arises if we can discover an evolution in the overall pattern of results that everyone, including the bookmakers, is missing.

There is little doubt that the games governing body, FIFA, is keen that football should have a few more goals. They were evidently upset that their showcase, the World Cup Finals in 1990, got perilously close to containing an average of just two goals in every game. Having seen their tentative proposals to increase the size of the goals go down in flames, they embarked on a back-door policy of getting the goal count up. This involved the stealthy introduction of changes that aided attackers, such as the back-pass rule and relaxing the offside law.

In 2000, they did something particularly sneaky - they changed the ball. In fact the introduction of the lighter ball for the European Championships and the following Premiership season characterises the fate of the tinkering of the rules-equipment that FIFA has indulged in. It could have been something else, or pure chance, but the number of goals during the competition suddenly got back to 2.7

per game (a high for the Championships), as was the intention. The lighter ball appeared to swirl around in a way that sometimes baffled goalkeepers. The Premiership season started with a flourish, easing past three goals per game in the first month... and then nothing. A miserable dribble of goals ensured that 2000-2001 remained stranded below 2.6 per game.

This pattern is a common feature of sudden changes to the overall structure of football. There is a period in which things go a little haywire, but before long everyone catches up and we're back to roughly the same statistical position we started with. Though certain patterns in the changes of results are gradual, a few can be very sudden indeed. The scourge of match fixing has long since gone, but increasingly the British game has become dogged with non-triers. But the phenomenon is very much in the punter's favour.

The amount of prestige attached to the winning of the various bits of silverware is changing constantly. In the mid-70s, the rarity of a live TV match was such that the FA Cup Final was a huge national treat. Now it slots uneasily with the other dozen or so matches from around the globe screened live on satellite and cable channels the same week. The European Champions League and domestic League Championship dominate the thoughts of the larger clubs, with the FA Cup wilting slightly.

But it is the League Cup (in whatever sponsorship guise it appears) that is the really fascinating competition for punters. In the late 90s, Manchester United dramatically scaled down their efforts to win the cup, culminating in a particularly extraordinary betting night for the third round on 13 October 1999.

For the visit of Bournemouth, West Ham (1-6 favourites) fielded a full-strength line-up and won 2-0. A few miles west, at Stamford Bridge, Chelsea (1-3) faced Huddersfield but with a side decidedly trimmed down of their usual first team. They lost 1-0. Though it is easy with hindsight, the 7-1 available on Huddersfield was a steal for anyone with the merest hint of how Chelsea's team sheet would look - a luxury not available to the bookies as they had to price the game two days before.

At Villa Park, Manchester United's effort only just deserved the label 'token', as their 'C' team lost 3-0 to Aston Villa (available at a rather generous 5-4 in the circumstances). By 2000, the uneasiness about whether the League Cup was really worth the effort had spread throughout the entire Premiership, and even to the top of the First Division. Paradoxically, Manchester United, stung by criticism of their withdrawal from the previous season's FA Cup, actually made an effort the following season, only adding to the confusion.

As a result, bookmakers tend to have to resort to some halfway house pricing. In the absence of knowing who may actually be turning up to play for Premiership teams, they conjure up a price somewhere between the one they would want to go with if it were a full strength team, and another if they knew it was only a sham. Amid this chaos, League Cup third round night is one of the great football punting events of the season.

Other sudden changes that effect betting markets are the referee directives on disciplinary matters from the FA . 'Get tough' policies or 'ease off' policies cause some of the greatest headaches for bookmakers, particularly spread betting firms. Bearing in mind the tendency I mentioned for a sudden change in the games stats to arrive with a flourish, only for things to return to their initial state, I would always look to avoid betting initially, as the information is accessible to all. In the case of a sudden increase in the number of cards being shown, it is almost certain to be a naturally better tactic to hold fire for perhaps a couple of weeks, let the furore die down and then look to go low on cards when the prices are high.

I have found there is a lot of mileage in only contemplating bets that appear to contradict what you can see happening with your own eyes. If trading in-running on a game where Arsenal are 2-0 ahead in 15 minutes, I would only look for reasons why the other team might be able to get back into the game. If I can't find any, I wouldn't trade. This might sound simply like trying to be different for the sake of it, but it is vital you force yourself to think in a different way to others.

Occasionally with football betting, this pattern is turned on its head, with everyone looking to ignore the obvious choice in favour of a voguish punt. This often happens with long-term bets, particularly pre-season betting on the divisional champions and the cup competitions. While Manchester United were dominating the Premiership in the 90s, most people were looking to try to find value in the other clubs, desperate as they were to pick the winner should Manchester United slip up.

In fact, looking back, the prices for United, around Evens, were still perhaps too generous. The FA Cup always seems to attract advice to bet on second-string teams from further down in the Premiership. The reasoning, that the top clubs are less motivated by the FA Cup, is sound; but if anything, the dominance of the Premiership elite in the last 10 years points to a tightening of the stranglehold of the top sides.

A lot of importance is attached to the statistics of individual clubs. At best these are not to be trusted; at worst they are a complete red herring. In many ways the term 'club' is a misnomer. Players move around so quickly that a side can change its entire playing staff, and get through two or more managers, in just a couple of seasons. To try to draw conclusions from games played in previous seasons has very little reliability. Statistics generally only demonstrate the broad patterns that are applicable to a side in their position. If Bolton were to top the First Division, winning 31 games in the process, the statistic tells us about the general ability of a side who wins the First Division, but it doesn't have any particular long-term relevance to Bolton in particular.

If, three years later, they are in the Premiership, it is clearly misleading to lump all Bolton's previous season's results together to suggest that they might have some predictive value. If they lie 14th in the Premiership, they now simply take on the statistical characteristics of a team that's 14th in the Premiership. Information about their reign at the top of a lower division is almost totally irrelevant.

TV pundits rarely attempt to give football betting tips. They are, however, keen to tell us the records between teams. Some of these records can seem quite startling. At the time of writing, Arsenal have beaten Leeds on five consecutive occasions and it is surprisingly common how many teams have not won against particular opponents for more than 10 games.

Buried in these figures may be a smattering of genuine information - particularly the fact that the closer the clubs geographically, the greater chance of an away win. But in general a strange pattern of results between teams is likely to be only a function of chance alone. There are over 8,000 combinations of teams amongst English league clubs. Among them are bound to be some very freaky looking records of previous games between any two clubs.

In 2001, I looked at the results between clubs where there was an eye-catching imbalance to their previous results and found no evidence that the previous head-to-head records were of any significance. Backing clubs where they had a history of winning the fixture did not increase returns over and above what could have been achieved by picking results at random.

## the friendless draw

Trying to predict the incidence of draws provided the backbone for much of football betting culture in Britain through the pools companies. It was no surprise that they used score draws as the basis of the entries as they are probably the most difficult of results to forecast. Draws can seem to have a mysterious life of their own, frustrating all attempts to seek them out. If you ask most people in what circumstances a draw occurs, they will probably tell you that it's something that happens when teams are evenly matched. To an extent this must be reasonably true, but the fundamental factor is, simply, that we use the word 'draw' to signify that two teams finished the match with the same number of goals. This rather obvious definition probably can't be extended much. Draws don't have a lot to do with teams being evenly matched. The likelihood of a draw is annoyingly anchored at close to 27 per cent for the vast majority of British league games. It is only where a team is significantly superior that this likelihood nudges down towards 24 per cent.

Draws are fundamentally connected with the number of goals that are expected - the lower the likelihood of goals, the greater the chances of a draw. Similarly the greater the number of goals, the less chance of the dreaded draw. (In a game containing 10 goals there is a vastly smaller chance of the teams ending on the same number as there is in a game containing just two goals). This explains why prices on the Scottish Third Division tend to be a couple of points better than in England. Goals fly in between teams of all abilities, as there isn't as much emphasis on conservative, defensive play. Two teams lying next to each other in the division are less likely to produce a draw than two seemingly well matched sides in the Premiership because they are naturally slightly more likely to go hammer and tongs at one another.

Draws are hopelessly under-represented in selections on most coupons, as they probably account for fewer than 10 per cent of all predictions even though they occur in more than a quarter of all matches. Their ability to strike when you least expect them is one of the greatest frustrations of football betting. It is important to try to find ways of softening their coupon-busting potential.

## bad habits

There are just a couple of areas where I feel that some football punters are particularly susceptible to being led astray. The first may cause a few raised eyebrows, but bad/dangerous habit no.1 is arbitrage, whether it be on spread betting or fixed-odds.

Arbitrage, the ability to trade in two directions on the same market in order to make an automatic profit, is often touted as a risk-free method of making money. It is anything but risk-free. It is a habit that can run smoothly for a long time - but there is a real, and often ignored, possibility of the whole thing blowing up in your face. The problem is that arbitrage encourages you to indulge in placing stakes that are huge compared to the amounts you are normally prepared to risk.

The ultimate arbitrage horror story that I've heard of happened to an account holder who thought he had traded a market successfully with two firms (at vast stakes) only to find the next day one of the firms voided his trade as a 'palpable error'. The legality of this was debatable, but you can imagine the despair of suddenly finding that one side of an arbitrage trade has suddenly disappeared leaving yourself massively at risk on the other. I have also seen account holders attempt to arbitrage with two firms on what they thought were identical markets, only to discover after the excitement had died down that the rules of each market were slightly different - i.e. *thinking* they were executing an arbitrage when one could not possibly have existed. This potentially could have led to massive losses with both firms.

A particularly time-consuming fantasy is that you can somehow arbitrage spread bets with fixed-odds bets. In the vast majority of cases you can't. You certainly can't arbitrage fixed-odds football bets with spread supremacy trades, no matter how vast the apparent difference in prices. Even if a team is rated at 1-2 with a fixed-odds firm but a spread company goes 1.0-1.3 supremacy for the other team (an unheard of disagreement), it is still impossible to stake in such a way as automatically to make a profit.

Fixed-odds arbitrage, taking prices with different firms on all results where the firms bet to 100 per cent, is less risky than its spread betting equivalent, but I would not encourage it as you tend to get into a mindset of constantly looking for such opportunities. Anyone with the patience to hunt around for such opportunities would probably be better off applying their skills to other areas of football betting.

The other bad, but understandable habit is that of indiscriminate betting, or more precisely, betting on a TV event 'because it's there'. I found out the significance of this by examining my own betting records. I discovered that bets placed between Monday and Friday produced a better return than those placed at the weekend. This situation is mirrored in the results of spread companies, who tend to be more profitable at weekends.

The explanation I received from one spread betting PR person was that the midweek trades tended to be placed disproportionately by 'clued-up' serious punters, including a handful of professional gamblers, who hoover up the best prices. The firms find the casual weekend punter easier to beat. This is probably essentially true, but I suspect that many individuals swing between being successful punters one day and then lapse into mug territory the next. This is because many gamblers do well midweek when there is no pressure to bet, and then give it back at the weekend when they feel obliged to enter into the spirit of a sporting Saturday.

The lesson is that the best bets tend to fall into your lap. If you find yourself saying "Is there anything to go on today?", then there probably isn't. A lot of gamblers suffer from the Sunday hangover effect of a winning Saturday. I know from bitter experience that bets on events on Sunday, particularly live matches, produce my worst results. The usual explanation for indiscriminate betting is that it is caused by people chasing losses. For me, it tends to be the other way around. After a loss I tend to become more tentative - it is following a large win that I tend to indulge in my most dubious betting.

chapter six

# going out on a limb

Having stated that the art of football betting largely comes down to thinking about information in a way that is significantly different to others, I'm going to indulge in the somewhat unfair game of presenting a single match plucked out of the air to illustrate the point. In doing so, I'm not particularly suggesting that the following betting principle is a route to riches in itself - but I reckon it provides a good example of the type of thinking that is vital in order to beat the odds. The match in question is the meeting of Everton and Coventry at Goodison Park on 2 October 1999. Using the traditional forecasting means, the following may have been taken into account.

Firstly league position: after nine games, Everton were lying sixth, Coventry 14th - so not a lot to indicate anything other than a home win. Current form appeared to give Everton a decisive advantage as well. In their last three league games they'd had a run of three straight wins, accounting for Sheffield Wednesday, West Ham and, in their previous fixture, managed a fantastic result by beating the local enemy Liverpool 1-0 at Anfield.

Coventry had won just two of their eight games of the season, losing two and winning one of their last three. How would a computer have coped with this information? It can't possibly see anything in the known information about the teams to forecast anything more than a solid home win. It simply has nothing to go on which could possibly point to any other result. Similarly, the most cursory of analysis by a non computer-aided person must reach the same conclusion.

William Hill odds were 8-13 Everton, 12-5 the draw, 4-1 Coventry. This gives us something more to go on. Hills' odds imply that there is a 61.9 per cent of a home win. It is possible that by applying all the data available we might come up with an estimate that is very slightly different. Bearing in mind Everton's fantastic run of recent form, we may even conclude that the odds on a home victory are too long.

This is the standard logic that most people would apply to the forecasting of sporting results. The bookies are using information to set the odds - perhaps if we can fine-tune the available information we might be able to emerge with an answer that is a slightly more accurate assessment of the odds on offer. If our assessment shows a significant variation from theirs, then there might be a betting opportunity. This is how the mechanics of most football forecasting work. In many instances it is probably a successful technique if refined precisely.

A thorough analysis of the corners market by the traditional means of looking at the recent spread make-ups of games involving the two clubs might be enough to beat the odds. But when it comes to betting on the results of individual games, I think we have to delve a good deal further into the stats.

The object of this delving is to try to discover any factor that appears to fly in the face of the usual analysis. Just as Mr Spock got hopelessly flummoxed when thing's became 'illogical', it is vital to find a factor that somehow contradicts the traditional view. The Everton v Coventry result was a 1-1 draw... it would have been too obvious to have plucked out an away win for the example!

In the case of this game, there is one thing that sticks out - the fact that Everton had come off a string of three consecutive victories. One of the first books I ever read on football betting suggested that "statistics show three victories is about the limit for most teams".

I assumed this was basically nonsense - the chance of consecutive victories simply diminishes naturally with every game. There could be no magical significance between a team winning its second, third or tenth game in a row, or so I thought. Is it possible that teams who win three times in a row reach a sort of mental barrier, their collective chests so puffed up that they can't motivate themselves to add a fourth scalp to the list?

To find out I looked at what happened to this exclusive band of teams in games following three consecutive victories. In the seasons spanning 1998 to 2000, there were 139 matches in which one of the teams came off the back of three wins or more. They actually didn't do as well as you might expect.

At home, 53 per cent of the teams won after an exceptional sequence, but this is not much better than any home team. When their next game was away for home they managed to win 29 per cent of the time, again not really spectacularly better than any old away team. If teams that won three or more in a row didn't seem to perform that well on their next trip out, could it be that those coming off the back of a run of three or more losses did slightly better than we might expect? In terms of percentage wins at home, they don't look too hot - with just a 37 per cent success rate.

As visitors, they achieved wins 27 per cent of the time (virtually the same as an average away team). In terms of beating their odds they performed very well, managing to rake up a theoretical profit of six per cent if you'd backed them all to level stakes.

Although the sample is not huge (seeing as winning or losing three or more games in a row is something of a rarity) the figures seem to demonstrate a bewildering fact. Fantastic teams, in terms of their recent form are probably, in betting terms, a very poor proposition.

Hopeless teams, on the other hand, are well worth backing. This odd conclusion is one of the more remarkable paradoxes of football betting. The principle crops up time and time again. The very thing that you would expect would contribute to a particular result seems to work against it.

To try to make sense of the 'three in a row phenomena', I began wondering about the psychological importance of certain numbers. For instance, it is well known that the number seven has a degree of significance. Seven lies at the limits of short-term memory. Most people can recall a seven-digit number a few seconds after it is presented to them, but it is extremely difficult to remember an eight-digit number.

I have always suspected that the difference between three and four is a similar type of threshold. Life can be a series of things that come in threes - bad luck supposedly adheres to this 'base three principle.

Sporting results might also tend to be thought in terms of series of three. Three straight victories constitute a particularly good achievement. Supporters can just about shrug off two consecutive losses, putting them down to short-term bad luck. If the run extends to three, the daggers start being sharpened and suddenly most members of the crowd decide that they would be better in the central defence than the present incumbents.

Amongst the most successful gamblers, across a number of sports, there is a semblance of a common theme. Going out on a limb doesn't necessarily mean backing teams at longer odds, though this is often attractive. It is very easy to find reasons why a team is going to win, but not as simple to conjure up good reasons why they won't. But forcing yourself to think negatively about a side's chances, particularly strong favourites, it is possible to stop seeing the game in black and white.

The seemingly astonishing results that occur every week no longer cause you any surprise. Having allowed this technique to influence your thinking, you are in good shape to start actually to predict where the shocks are coming next.

chapter **seven**

# disrupting the home/away balance

Many aspects of football betting revolve around the leagues' home/away balance - the overall expected frequencies of a home win, draw and away win. There are short-term fluctuations but in general, throughout the English leagues (Scotland varies considerably) we can be reasonably certain that, at the end of the year, close to 47 per cent of all the games will have resulted in a home win, 27 per cent as draws and 26 per cent as away wins.

Trying to fathom out why there is such a vast difference between the performance of home and away teams is like piecing together the clues from a whodunit. The factors are interlinked, so trying to isolate them is particularly difficult, but the home/away balance is so fundamental that a thorough understanding has to be the basis for any strategy.

Since we can identify a template on which a division is based, we can also say that this 47-27-26 percentage split is the best estimate of the three outcomes in a game in which the two teams are evenly matched. The odds that roughly correspond to these percentages are 11-10 for a home win, 11-4 for both the draw and the away win. Account for the bookies' margin of just over 10 per cent and the actual odds offered for a match between two clubs of equal ability is close to 10-11 a home win; 12-5 the draw and the away win. Adjusting the home/away balance in the odds reflects the relative merits of each team, so a slightly better than average home side will be offered at 4-6, a slightly worse than average away team at 3-1.

We know that in British amateur football there is virtually no home/away split. A Sunday league team going to the neighbouring village has about the same chance of winning as if the game was played on their own turf. This means that we can probably dismiss any notion that the split is due to the difference in playing surfaces, pitch dimensions, etc. In general, the better the standard of football, the greater the home/away split.

The other variable that fluctuates depending on the standard of play is the number of goals. These decrease as the standard rises. At the absolute bottom end of the scale, a couple of school teams can frequently chalk up more than 10 goals in substantially fewer than 90 minutes. During the finals of the World Cup, where you'd imagine technical skill was at its highest, the goal count is lower than in any group of games that can be classed together, hardly nudging past more than two per game in recent times.

If it's not the pitches that turn the away side into a quivering mass, then perhaps it's the supporters. Having 30,000 home fans baying for your blood is enough to put off anyone. In principle this must hold, though the relationship between the size of the home crowd and result of the game is not quite as clear cut as we might expect. If there is a direct correlation between the number of fans and home success, then we would expect the best attended games (in the Premiership) to produce the highest proportion of home wins.

In fact the home/away split is slightly more pronounced in the First to Third divisions than in the Premiership. Though the differences between the English divisions are fairly insignificant, you would have thought that the partisan atmosphere of a 40,000 capacity at Stamford Bridge had a more adverse effect on the visitors performance than the 2,500 who can be expected to support Torquay.

The division that is completely out on a limb from the rest of the British game is Scottish Division Three. Here the home advantage is tiny, along with the crowds. Home advantage counts for little compared to the bubbling cauldron of the Premiership.

Hosts enjoy virtually no advantage at all, so a template of closer to 38 per cent for both teams and 24 per cent for the draw must be applied to the games. So two equally matched teams in this division should attract odds of around 13-8, whereas the odds for two equally-rated Premiership clubs will probably be skewed 10-11 for the home side and 12-5 for the visitors.

Overall in 2000-2001, 37 per cent of Scottish Division Three matches resulted in away wins. Intriguingly where games attracted no more than a handful of spectators, the home side's form collapsed completely. In 32 games where there was an attendance of fewer than 290, just seven home sides won. Sides with low home attendance are probably quite naturally poor anyway, but they still appeared to be overestimated in their odds, as £10 on all these games to be away wins racked up a return of £450. In general there is very little margin for the bookies in away wins in Scottish Division Three, to the extent that in some years, notably 1999-2000, there was a theoretical profit in backing all the away sides throughout the season.

The relationship between decibels of the home crowd and the result is quite intriguing. There is little doubt that the introduction of all-seater stadiums has had an impact on the atmosphere of football matches. Even with crowds over 20,000, it takes a lot to stir up the home fans. When Leeds were in the First Division in the 80s, Elland Road still had a bank of terracing, and the intimidation factor must have been considerable. Today their own supporters admit that the decibel level is a fraction of yesteryear.

In the last couple of seasons, I have witnessed plenty of times where there was considerably more noise from the away section of a ground. In the days of terracing, the die-hard vocal supporters would gather at one end and give the opposition some collective stick. But football has successfully marketed itself to appeal to a broader section of people. With the number of families attending live football, and a decidedly more upmarket social profile, the screaming nutters have been swallowed up in the vast new stadia.

If we accept that modern day grounds are no longer the sorts of places where visiting players are significantly put off, then it should show in the results. But there is absolutely no sign that away teams are faring any better than when they were lucky to come away from some grounds with their limbs intact.

The appointment of Sven Goran Ericksson as England manager may spell the start of a significant shift towards applying scientific and psychological principles in the constant quest to improve the performance of players. In the absence of any identifiable reasons, perhaps the issue of why travelling sides do so badly will receive more attention. In the meantime watch out for any patterns in British football that suggest visiting teams are making up ground.

Of all clubs, Wimbledon are establishing a semi-permanent record of better results on the road. Currently homeless, having to play at Selhurst Park where a huge swath of the seating is reserved for away fans, the Dons appear to have no fear of leaving their home turf. Indeed, away results seem to indicate they are causing difficulties for the odds compilers.

In 2000-2001, although finishing well outside the play-off places, they only lost six out of 23 games away. Backing them to draw or win in each of their games would have produced a profit of two and eight points respectively. I don't believe this is a case of just picking out a team at random on the basis of a spurious short-term pattern of results. I suspect that before long a number of clubs will realise that there is an opportunity to be had in persuading players that they are not naturally handicapped when playing away. Over the course of years the imbalance may start to right itself.

# local derbies

Having said that small, quiet crowds tend to favour the home side, there is a wealth of evidence that in some matches where the attendance leaps, there is also a strong advantage to the away team. Local derbies are a feature of football the world over, and the sudden lack of the usual supremacy of the home team is replicated in all the international leagues.

Trying to define a derby game is not always easy - traditional rivalries persist but these can gain or decrease in intensity over the course of a number of seasons. Each geographical area of the country has its own pattern. Local clubs can get stuck together in the same division (Torquay, Plymouth and Exeter battling it out in the Third Division was an example from 2000-2001). Some clubs, however, get stranded from their local rivals by the process of promotion and relegation, possibly making rivalries less intense over time. A good example of this is Grimsby Town who, by pushing into the First Division for a long period, have managed to show a clean pair of heels to Lincoln, Scunthorpe and Hull.

Bad relations between clubs can spring up quickly. Alex Ferguson and Kevin Keegan (then of Newcastle) had a memorable public spat that significantly raised the temperature between clubs. The evidence of this can be seen in the high bookings make-ups in Manchester United-Newcastle games since.

Geographical proximity isn't everything. A local pecking order can be established whereby the team at the bottom of the pile (in terms of prestige) most vehemently hates the next team up, though it doesn't necessarily work the other way around. Notts County aren't too keen on Forest, but Forest apparently see County as a little brother type outfit who aren't worth their wrath.

Leeds are bothered with Manchester United, though they're not strictly particularly close in miles; Bradford get in a lather over Leeds and, for many years, Derby, following a managerial row in the early 80s. However, they couldn't care less about Halifax, just down the road. The First Division has recently been infested by a clutch of North-West teams. There are a complex web of rivalries between Blackburn, Preston, Bolton, Manchester City, Burnley and Stockport. This swarm of North-West teams has contributed to a general impression that Bolton could be the most disliked club in the county in terms of being cited as rivals by the most clubs, though many will have alternative ideas. Celtic v Rangers is by far the most poisonous relationship between two clubs in the UK, though Swansea and Cardiff are capable of stirring up plenty of trouble in their meetings.

In the last Premiership season, there were 32 games that could be identified as derbies - 12 were home wins, 11 draws and nine away wins. The extraordinary proportion of draws is not exceptional for such games. Part of the reason for this lies in the fact that derbies tend to contain fewer goals than average (just 2.2). Fewer goals always means a greater proportion of draws, as it is far more likely that both teams will finish on the same number.

This small sample actually contained a large number of goals, even though the draw count was very high. It could be that in particularly tense games, teams tend to be keener to settle for a draw, even if it's comparatively high one like 2-2. For these games, betting level stakes on every away side would have required a stake of 32, returning 31; so here the odds on the away team were just short enough to ensure that you couldn't make an automatic profit. Draws returned 37 points for the same 32-point stake, easily beating the odds.

A similar pattern occurs whichever derby games you examine. There are fewer home wins and more draws. In fact such is the frequency of draws that they consistently beat the odds. In the 1999-2000 season, I looked at the results of the 68 games that I considered being the fiercest derby games: 29 were drawn (43 per cent), with only 27 (40 per cent) resulting in a home win - an extraordinary imbalance.

Despite my comments about the possibility of teams settling for a draw, I am always slightly suspicious when a relatively small sample of matches contains either an inflated or decreased number of draws. Because they tend to be such a constant, stuck between 26 and 30 per cent, any radical departure from this frequency can suggest that the number of games in the sample is too small to be considered truly representative.

The one figure that does appear to be constant is the lowered 40 per cent success rate for home sides in derbies. This was confirmed when I examined the records of London Premiership sides playing each other over the last seven seasons. The draw and away frequencies bobble around, so that at any one time, either result can seem undervalued in the betting. My conclusion is that going against the home side in a derby is a sound strategy, but on the fixed-odds I can't be sure whether there is any particular value in backing the draw. A safer bet is to sell the home team on the spreads so not pinning yourself to a precise draw or away win prediction.

Looking at the pattern of results in derbies, it does seem as though local rivalries seem to benefit away sides that are naturally 'inferior' to their hosts. Without wishing to suggest that Charlton are inferior to West Ham, it is clear that they are historically not quite the same status as near neighbours. In a derby situation, this appears to benefit the underdog. Charlton would tend to raise their game more at Upton Park than West Ham would at The Valley.

It is noticeable that many of the away wins achieved at very long odds are in games where a 'lowly' local visitor takes the points unexpectedly. It was 7-1 Charlton who pulled of one of the more startling Premiership away wins by beating Chelsea in 2000-2001. This seems to make some sense bearing in mind the previously mentioned upward rivalry where the 'lesser' team are more strung up about the rivalry than the bigger brother.

Clearly a short trip appears to benefit the away team, so could it be that a longer trip might benefit the home side. This interesting possibility has been raised by the betting analyst and former professional footballer Terry Norman. According to the theory, in certain circumstances away teams are disadvantaged because they have to endure a gruelling journey to their opponents. This is particularly applicable to the hard-up lower league clubs who cannot afford to stay overnight during the week in hotels and therefore make the round trip in a single day/night.

Certain journeys between clubs are particularly awful in the UK. Anywhere to Plymouth isn't a lot of fun - Plymouth and Hartlepool are the two most geographically isolated teams in Britain. In 2000-01, Plymouth had a remarkably skewed home/away record, winning 13 out of 23 at home (a better than average tally) but only winning twice away from home (much worse). They routinely seem to beat far away Carlisle (a run of eight consecutive wins in recent years). Darlington have a similarly abnormal record against Exeter.

I have often attempted a definitive analysis of the travellers' phenomena only to run up against a host of problems in knowing how to handle the data fairly. I was recently looking at the pattern of results in other countries and discovered that the home/away balance is occasionally greater overseas than it is here. The one county where home wins manage to break the 50 per cent barrier is Russia, where the distances between clubs are greater than just about anywhere else in the international leagues.

There are a number of occasions in British and European football where attendances are minimal and the degree of competitiveness is considerably lower than at other times. These are always worth looking out for to find an away win fest. I have always been a little suspicious of the odds for the first round of the Scottish League Cup - played very early in the season at the beginning of August, or even late July. In terms of lack of spectators, the early legs of this competition beat all records for British football.

On 31 July 1999, the first round tie between Clydebank and East Stirling attracted just 69 paying spectators. This tells us quite a lot about the attractiveness, and possibly competitiveness, of ties on that day. It would be fair to say that in these games home advantage counts for almost nothing - the 'roar of the crowd' to motivate the home side is patently lacking. There were just three home wins in 12 first round matches in 1998, and none at all in 1999.

A similarly low-key series of matches exists in England in the form of the cup competition for the lower league teams. In recent years, this has taken the guise of the LDV Trophy, AutoWindscreens Shield, etc depending on the sponsors. The first round games generally take place in early December.

There are two characteristics that work in favour of backers of away teams. As in the Scottish League Cup, the distinct lack of prestige of the competition keeps the fans away, eroding the natural advantage of the hosts. In addition, competition is played on a north/south regional basis to cut down the burden of long distance travelling expenses. Consequently, there is a slight 'local derby' factor at work in many games that aids the away sides.

There is a marked tendency for away sides to perform better than when they are playing league games. My records suggest that the bookies don't sufficiently take this into account, to the extent that amongst the past five competitions, only in 2000 would you have made a loss by exclusively backing away teams in the first round. The analysis of small numbers of games is fraught with danger. It is very easy to jump to conclusions too early and dream up biases in the odds which, long-term, don't really exist at all. In the European Champions League in 1994, there were murmurings that home sides felt so pressured to perform in front of their huge partisan home crowd that they were performing quite poorly.

This was given as the explanation by the TV pundits for a particularly freak run of away wins. In 2000, all the talk was of the complete invincibility of the home sides, following their complete dominance of the years' group rounds of the competition. These conclusions were reached on the basis of a quite small sample of games and could easily be the product of pure chance.

chapter **eight**

# no shortcuts to value

The last day of the Premiership campaign is supposed to be a nerve-tingling finale to the football season where, even if the destination of the championship is already known, there are relegation and European qualification issues to be resolved. But in 2001, with Manchester United on a different planet to the rest of the division, the destination of the trophy had been decided weeks beforehand and, at the foot of the table, the fates of Coventry, Bradford and Manchester City had been sealed.

This left us with just one game of real significance. Liverpool had to win at Charlton to secure a place in the following season's Champions League. The significance of this game from a betting angle is that it offers a window on trying to understand the key concept of value betting.

The use of the term 'value' in gambling is as problematic as it's over-employment in shop window displays. It became the vogue term with the publication of *Value Betting* by Mark Coton- a classic treatise on how the core method of beating the bookie was only to bet when the odds on offer were above those of the true chance of the runner winning. If you had achieved a value bet, it was somewhat irrelevant whether it won or not. Over the long run a series of value bets must produce a profit, regardless of the number or frequency of winners.

The basis of the theory is acceptable to most gamblers, but some of the implications of the 'value is king' argument are lost on people. The Charlton v Liverpool game illustrates why. Liverpool faced this crucial game just three days after a gruelling UEFA Cup final in Holland, finally beating Alaves with a golden goal in extra-time after a thrilling 4-4 draw. Their success in winning the UEFA Cup, Coca-Cola Cup and FA Cup had required them to play more games than any other Premiership side, many fixtures piling up towards the end of the season.

To many, the *Racing Post* included, Liverpool were liable to suffer an almighty hangover - in the footballing sense, if not literally. Charlton were offered at 3-1, an extraordinarily long price for a home team. The sound argument went that the price would have been fair had Liverpool come into the game relatively fresh, but the jaded Liverpool had more than the 25 per cent chance of losing at the Valley.

Let's say two punters, Bill and Ben, had taken opposing views. Bill had money on the 'value' option, a Charlton win; Ben couldn't see past Liverpool at 4-5 (value or no value). Had Bill been right and Liverpool been turned over, then there is no debate. Bill would have landed a value win - Ben's bet would have been consigned to the loser's pile.

But in reality events panned out differently. Liverpool showed absolutely no signs of fatigue and eased to a 4-0 victory. Which of our fictitious punters should be joyous, and why? Ben, on Liverpool at around 4-5, is going to the pay-out counter, but did he have the better bet? If value is the only key factor, then the answer must still be... no, he didn't. This is hard for many to swallow. We may accept there is such a thing as a good, possibly unlucky, losing bet - but the concept of a bad winning bet is quite alien.

But that is exactly what the bet on Liverpool was. In the circumstances, it seems clear that the Reds should have been a shade of odds against, possibly 6-5. The moment a bet was struck at 4-5, Ben was effectively on a loser, whatever the result. Of course the assertion that Charlton shouldn't have been as high as 3-1 is very contentious, but it is useful to imagine that, somewhere out there, there was a 'correct' estimation of what odds the teams should have been priced at. An example of a situation where we are mathematically sure of the true chances of success helps illustrate the situation.

When a coin is flipped we can only guess at the result, but we absolutely know that the true odds of either a head or a tail are Evens. The moment you have a tenner on heads at 4-5, you are a losing punter. You have just handed the bookie a 10 per cent margin, the difference between the £20 he should have paid you if the odds were fair and the £18 he actually pays you, if you guess correctly.

The result of the next flip really makes no difference to this equation. If you strike a bad value bet, you get simply get paid less than you should. In the long-term the bookies' margin will take its toll on your betting funds, even though the number of times you win might be the same, or perhaps more than, a successful value seeker.

The unease with the apparent contradiction of value betting - that you can 'lose' even if you win - has led to an unfortunate watering down of this key betting fundamental. Nowadays there is talk of finding "winners at value prices". Here the emphasis moves onto finding a winner and then worrying about getting the best price.

This confuses the scene completely. Value is solely about getting prices that are better than the true chance. Consider the following set of prices to win the Premiership - Manchester United 10-11, Liverpool 4-1, Arsenal 4-1, Chelsea 66-1. If you were asked, "Which is the most likely team to win the Premiership?" - the only sensible answer can be Manchester United. Only the most die-hard Chelsea fan would have any realistic hopes of them breaking United's stranglehold.

Clearly their hopes are faint, but at 66-1 it could be argued that they are not as hopeless as the 1.49 per cent as the odds suggest. Perhaps their true chances are in the range of 3-4 per cent. Chelsea appear to be on offer at a value price, despite the fact that the moment we place money on them we have no realistic expectation of ever picking up. In this somewhat unrealistic example the only bet is on Chelsea, even though it would appear to take strong will.

I am deliberately stretching the value argument, which applies to spread betting. This crops up with the much repeated argument, "Nobody ever got poor by taking a profit." This phrase tends to be the defence for those who frequently close spread bets.

It is on this subject that the value argument reaches its critical point. Personally, I try to avoid closing spread bets unless I'm convinced that there is value to be had on the closing of the trade as well as its opening. This is a very rare situation. If you think a spread is too high at some stage and sell the market, then the impression tends to remain that it keeps high throughout, whatever happens on the field of play in the meantime.

The whole concept of value seems to be undergoing a painful reassessment recently. On a practical level, it is the case that very few punters, including quite successful ones, evaluate value in the text book fashion of examining odds and then only betting on the option that appears to have been generously priced.

What usually happens is that we identify a particular side we want to back for whatever reason, and then get the cash down fairly irrespective of its price. If we pick our selections in a particularly unique way, we find value all the time anyway - so we hardly need to bother about the prices on offer. But as a general rule, I still tend towards the adage of 'find the value and the winners will take care of themselves'.

chapter **nine**

# the shape of current form

When we study a team's form, we assume there must be some basic rules about how what has happened to them in the past will affect them in the future. We don't tend to question the fact that if Millwall have a blistering recent record, they are more liable to win their next game; similarly, Blackpool's appalling run of form can only indicate they are in for a pasting next time. But if we apply the same logic to everyday life it is possible to see that the fact something has happened in the past doesn't necessarily mean it will repeat in the future; indeed, there are a variety of situations where common sense tells us that something happening in the past makes its reoccurrence very unlikely.

Imagine there is a wonky paving stone that has gone unrepaired in your local high street. Such is its danger potential that one in 2,000 people who walk on that particular pavement will trip on it, possibly causing a minor injury. One Saturday morning you fall victim to it and are sent crashing. When you walk past the same spot on Monday morning, now wary of the hazard, what is the chance of the same thing happening again? Unless you are hopelessly unobservant we would hope it is only a minuscule possibility, much less than the 2,000-1 chance that everyone else has of coming a cropper. Here, the occurrence of one event (tripping over) directly leads to a substantial decrease in the chance of it happening again.

To a certain extent this applies to any sports where humans are the competitors, rather than animals. The fact that human footballers are a mass of different emotions and motivations makes the study of football form significantly different than horse racing. To what extent horses 'know' they have just won or lost is debatable, but we can assume they don't go through the same mental agonies as footballers and their managers.

Footballers are acutely aware of the significance of certain patterns of results. Clearly they are sensitive to the result of the last meeting of two clubs and tend to make a special effort not to let a particular opponent do the double (winning home and away) in a season. Every game brings a different scenario - one team may be on a run of bad results, another side may have had their hopes rise following the signing of a new player, another may have just lost their manager. Every game comes with a different set of emotional baggage.

At the end of the season a team finishes in a particular position in the league. This is the sum of their efforts, the ultimate indicator of their performance in the last nine months. Each match result adds one more piece of evidence to the overall scene. I think there is a definite way in which looking at a team's performance is good from a betting angle. If Stoke are lying fifth in the table and their opponents, Gillingham, are 14th, most punters will use this information at face value to predict the result. Whether it be by a guess or a precise study of previous results, they will tend to look for the 'correct' answer to the question, "What should happen when a fifth-placed team meets a side in 14th place?" Attempting to be ultra-accurate, they may conclude that Stoke have a 46 per cent chance of winning the match.

To develop the mindset of a winning punter it is much better to turn the argument on its head and say, "Is there a reason why this match should be different from one in which a fifth-placed team is up against a 14th placed team?" If the answer is no, then I rarely bother examining it further.

The first time I realised current form was something that couldn't be looked at in a rigid way was when I altered my technique for picking away selections. In 1991, I had a freaky run of success by picking teams from the lower divisions to win at prices of between 3-1 and 9-2. On one particular Saturday, I managed to find six straight winners, backing them in trebles, paying around 80-1 on the total stake. The very next week, using the same technique, I found another four, which this time I backed in an accumulator. At that time the monetary value seemed vast (though only about £1,200), and brimming with confidence, I decided that I should try to tweak a seemingly winning strategy in order to squeeze out more profits.

The original technique had been to look for evidence that the away team's current form was out of step with its league position. Assuming prices were set roughly according to a side's position in the league, I set about finding whether there was an imbalance in the team's recent form. To achieve this I used the team's relative tally of points as a measure of their strength and then looked at the last four games to see whether their current form was broadly representative of a team in their league position - or significantly better or worse.

This involved rating each side's previous four opponents. So a mid-table team should have an 'average' performance over their last four games. This was all expressed in numerical terms. For games they had won they would be allocated a strength rating based on the overall points tally of the team they had beaten. A draw or loss would be accounted for in a similar way. Having taken the home/away balance into account the model produced a rating for each team depending on their recent performance compared to their league position. The best betting situation occurred when the home team was riding high in the table but having a run of comparatively bad form against a team who were down the table but experiencing a run of good form.

There was, however a logical problem with the set-up. Because I was compiling the information for the weekend some days in advance, I wasn't taking into account the fixtures that took place on Tuesday and Wednesday . Despite the fact that I was ahead, it did seem somewhat absurd to have a system based on current form that was not using the results from many of the club's games immediately prior to the ones I was trying to forecast. Having decided I would clearly have to do this in future, I realised there was a particular significance to midweek games. As the bookies try to have the weekend coupons in their shops by Tuesday at the latest, they had to price the Saturday matches before many teams had played in midweek.

In terms of the potential to beat the odds, midweek games must have had enormous importance... or so I thought. The easiest way to find a team who were undervalued in the odds for their Saturday game must simply be to see how they'd done midweek. Rather than trawling through mountains of stats, it had to make sense that a particularly good or poor midweek result was a key pointer to whether or not a team's current form was worthy of their league position.

On the basis of this minor revelation it became clear that, to gain an advantage on Saturday, it made sense to back a team that, on paper, was relatively poor, if it had managed a surprise win, particularly away from home, a few days earlier. If there was a fixture where the opposition was basically good but had experienced a poor midweek result, particularly a home loss, then the combination afforded the opportunity for a great value bet on the team the odds implied were the outsiders.

I distinctly remember the first September weekend I put the theory into practice. Having found seven away sides fitting the bill on that week's coupon, I covered them with 35 trebles and looked forward to the results expectantly. I managed to pick six home winners and one miserable draw. This pattern set in with a vengeance - a hopeless series of losing bets.

Going back to the drawing board it seemed, bizarrely, as if current form information was sufficient to beat the odds, but only if you discounted the last game. Even more weird was the fact that if you included the last game into the current form assessment it seemed as if the tactic produced forecasts that were so off the mark it was actually better long-term to bet against what the logical assessment of current form seemed to indicate.

It took a long time to figure out what lay behind this strange phenomenon. In the meantime the tactic of trying to pick winners in the 3-1 to 9-2 price bracket was being scuppered by other forces. The slight bias towards those who were willing to take a risk with longer shots had, by the mid-90s, disappeared - as the home teams became better natural value. Along with tax, this meant there was too much ground for away-win enthusiasts to make up, and I began looking elsewhere, mostly speciality bets , and in particular spread betting. But with the availability of tax-free betting towards the end of the decade, I started to look again at the problems I had encountered with current form.

I became interested in the study of current form sequences presented by Bill Hunter in his book *Football Fortunes*. The basis of these is a vast analysis (39,000 sequences, called triads, over 10 years) which looks at how various combinations of results effect the outcome of a game. So, for example, a team coming into the game off the back of a home win and then an away loss has, according to Hunter's figures, a 47.39 per cent chance of winning their next home match. The current form dyad (the previous two results) of the home team could be matched with the away side's dyad. By looking at the record of games where this pairing of dyads had previously come together it would be possible to arrive at a good estimate of the current game.

In broad terms I was suspicious of this approach because it appeared as if it would throw back answers that we could have guessed at with considerably less legwork. Obviously, it seemed, certain patterns of previous results were quantifiably better than others. A team can have six previous results, (HW, HD, HL, AW, AD, AL). Some sequences of two must constitute better than average current form - e.g. HW (home win) followed by AW (away win). Such teams playing at home should achieve greater success than the 47 per cent of home teams who win generally. Likewise, the sequence HD (home draw) followed by AL (away loss) was somewhat worse than average, so we might expect the chance of winning their preceding home game to be slightly less than the 47 per cent average.

Though the author makes no more than general comments on the findings, there are, buried away in the tables, a number of figures that blew away the traditional forecasting view I had previously held. The sequence 'HW, AL' can be thought as the standard sequence - a sort of baseline. In the first game, where the team won at home, this was by far the most likely result. When they lost in the next game this too was the most obvious result - so nothing particularly interesting has happened - their last two games were very average affairs. This, logically enough, leads to a very average result for their following home game. In matches where the home team brings the current form of HW, AL to the game, the result is a home win 47.39 per cent of the time. So no surprise there.

Now consider the sequence of HL, AW immediately before a home game. Here both results were as surprising as you can get, with the most recent one, the away win, the best possible result out of the six that a team can bring to their next game. I would say that this sequence demonstrates somewhat better recent form than the previous example of HW, AL. Assuming this is the case, then the result of their next home game should be slightly better than average - i.e. the proportion of home wins in games following the sequence HL, AW might be expected to be greater than 47.38 per cent.

The trouble is, the figure is actually 44.15 per cent. This may not seem such a dramatic difference, but considering the size of the sample it is almost certainly very significant. We know that the proportion of home wins stays doggedly stuck in the high 40s - any series of matches in British leagues that deviates by more than a few percent from this baseline is relatively odd. Here we have particularly low figure that is associated with teams that have just achieved the best of all possible results in their last game.

This finding started the process of fitting the jigsaw together. Winning may not be all it's cracked up to be. In particular, winning your last game away from home possibly blunts a team's ability to win their next home game. Here we are getting the first signs that there is an element of 'reverse psychology' in evidence.

Over the past couple of years, I have examined how the recent record of teams may effect the result. The results seem to demonstrate that league position is, in general, a much better indicator of a team's ability to win rather than their recent form - though there are some slightly unexpected conclusions that are well worth bearing in mind. My studies have mainly concentrated on 'ordinary' games - those where the home team is a shade under Evens and the away side in the 11-4 to 4-1 bracket. In such games we might expect a rough 50-50 split between those home teams who win and those who don't. What I was particularly looking for was any evidence that the current form of the teams coming into these types of matches was in any way different for games that resulted in home wins, compared to those which didn't.

Awarding points to sides on the basis of their results in the past four games (three for a win, one for a draw) resulted in finding the average number of points that a team had won in their last four games. This was 5.8 points. The degree of variation amongst them was enormous. Many teams in the Evens price bracket come into home games off the back of very poor form. It is quite common to find a team rated at odds-on for a home match where they have failed to win in their previous four games. Similarly, away sides can attract a quote of well over 3-1, even though they are unbeaten for a considerable spell.

I looked to discover whether splitting the sample into those who won their next game from those who didn't would reveal if there was anything in their form that hinted at what the result of the next game might have been. But the average form for homes teams who subsequently lost was exactly the same, 5.8. This seems to demonstrate that the recent record a home team brings to a game is of very little predictive value.

Another possibility is that when the away team has better current form than the home side they have an increased chance of success. Strangely, this too is not the case. Of games where the home team had won, about 60 per cent had better current form than their opponents. But this figure of 60 per cent remained rock solid among those who had failed to win as well. So we can't necessarily say that an away team with better current form than their opponents have any advantage.

In fact I have performed all sorts of analytical tricks on the figures to see whether there is any relationship between the difference in both side's current form and the result of a subsequent game, and I'm afraid there doesn't seem to be much semblance of a pattern. But that, largely, is the end of the bad news.

In terms of the number of tactical decisions they have to make, there is a slight difference between home and away sides. Home sides are expected to win - they have to score at least one goal. Since the away side would tend to consider a draw to be a good result, they have a fairly definite choice of whether to sit back while they are still level or go forward with some commitment. This, in association with some supporting figures, makes me think that perhaps the record of the away team, taken in isolation, is a better predictor of results than looking at what the home team has to offer, or the difference between the form of the two.

Going back to the analysis of current form, there appears to be a pattern whereby away sides with a good recent record tend to do relatively well whatever the opposition's record. Where the away team has accumulated eight points or more in their last four games, it appears to decrease the frequency of home wins to 40 per cent, much lower than the average.

This would seem to suggest that away sides with a positive outlook - e.g. those with good recent form- could blunt the natural supremacy of home teams, regardless of who the home team is, or what their form looks like. Since we assume that the natural supremacy of the home team is mostly in the head, rather than related to any tangible factor, this appears to possess some logic. In a sense, home sides are somewhat robotic. They play to the same level whatever the circumstances. I'm tempted to say it is the outlook of away sides that actually plays more part in determining the result. The betting consequences of this are quite strange.

If you take a home team with very poor recent record against a semi-moderate away outfit, it might look as though there is a distinct advantage to the visitors. Buy in general, I would say this may not be the case. However, when a basically good home side comes up against a basically good away side, the visitors tend to be undervalued in the betting.

My original tactic of backing away teams whose form was out of step with their league position came off the rails seemingly because of the last result of the teams. I had assumed that teams who won midweek would have a natural advantage against those who had lost. This is where most things we assume about football forecasting fly straight out of the window.

There appears to be a 'cornered animal' scenario that applies to the strongest sides. At what point is a high-flying side at their most dangerous? In a traditional forecasting sense, the answer must be, "After they've just hammered someone." But it would appear the one time you don't want to meet a decent outfit is just after they've lost.

I have looked at the results of games immediately after teams in the top three of their division had suffered a rare defeat. In these games their average goal supremacy over the opposition is actually about 0.2 better than their usual performance. Amassing a huge sample of such games is difficult, as top teams simply don't lose that often. But subjectively, a few patterns seem to stand out.

As a predictor of when a top team is likely to thrash their opponents, an unexpected defeat in the previous game seems to contain many warning signs. I examined what happened to teams immediately before they went on to win by at least four goals. Teams that win by four goals at any time are likely to be fundamentally good teams, so we might expect their last match result was at least as good as average. In fact big wins have a slight tendency to follow disappointing results.

The 'bouncy ball' tendency of teams to follow a good result/bad result pattern is particularly evident following an FA Cup giant-killing. As a rule, always look to oppose a side that has just managed a terrific result in a cup competition, especially if it was achieved against opponents from a higher division. The hangover effect in their next league game tends to be pronounced, leading to a worse-than-expected performance. At the other end of the scale, I have a feeling that lower division sides who lose heavily against more illustrious opponents tend to do better than expected when they go back to their divisional games.

With the ever-increasing turnover of managers there has been some speculation as to whether a club's results improve after a change in management. At present the voguish answer is that they don't. This followed some research at a Dutch University in 2000 that seemed to contradict the assumption that sacking a manager was the best way of improving results quickly. Trying to measure whether sacking a manager works in terms of the team doing better is fraught with difficulties.

The Dutch report concluded, bizarrely, that although there seemed to be a slight improvement following the appointment of a new manager, this could be put down to the fact that the standard of opposition was worse in the games following the sacking/resignation.

This takes a lot of thinking about - but in terms of betting, the only fact we need to know is whether there is a profit to be had in backing teams that have just changed their manager. Some very interesting results from *www.football-punter.co.uk* seem to indicate this is the case. This seems logical enough. A team who has just lost their manager will have probably suffered a dreadful run of results, upon which the odds are based. Since their stock is low anyway, one major upheaval, whether it be a change of management or another factor, is quite likely to shift things slightly their way, making them a reasonable bet.

Perhaps the most potent aspect of motivational factors in football is the situation where one team is suddenly suffering a personnel crisis. I have always become excited when hearing that an entire club has been struck down with flu and are struggling to turn out 11 fit players. On the face of it, this seems a perfect opportunity to get on their opponents as the information is unlikely to be assimilated into the odds.

But again, the results seem to indicate that the common sense bet is not necessarily the best. I have made a note of the dozen or so bets I've had in the last few seasons on the basis of an illness stricken squad. The results are awful - a loss of 40 per cent. It just may be that a 'B' team, in a moment of crisis for the club, manages to play well above their natural ability levels, actually beating their odds.

This situation, however, is probably only very short-term. The effect of a growing injury list is probably fully reflected in the odds for games, though the loss of key influential players may not be. In terms of beating the odds, the loss of central defenders appears as if it may be relatively ignored compared to the loss of key attackers. But it is usually the shape of the back line that has a disproportionate effect on the results of a team, particularly if the captain is a central defender. The advice here is to get on the opponents of sides afflicted with the loss of the backbone of their defence, but pay less attention to injuries elsewhere.

In terms of a player who a side can least afford to lose, my stats indicate that it is the regular goalkeeper who has a disproportionate effect in holding a team together. The loss of the first team keeper causes results to dip alarmingly, to the extent that a theoretical profit can be made backing against any side forced to draft in a reserve goalkeeper.

chapter **ten**

# assessing a team's strength

If we ask the question, "How good is a team?", there are two measurements we can use, neither of which gives a particularly accurate picture. Football pundits will tend to use one or other, depending on which paints a more dramatic picture. So we might hear that "Brighton have only picked up three points in their last eight games" or "Blackburn have scored 15 goals in their last three outings".

It may seem that it doesn't really matter how we express a team's performance, but there are subtle differences between the two yardsticks of 'points won' and 'goals scored'. As far as the teams are concerned, it is the points they win that are obviously of prime importance.

In some ways the allocation of points doesn't accurately reflect how good a team is. Winners get three points and a draw earns just one. The imbalance of a three-to-one ratio was introduced to try to discourage draws. It hasn't really worked, as the frequency of draws remains stubbornly high. The fact that a win is deemed to be three times better than a draw means the allocation of points hugely magnifies the importance of winning.

If you look at the record of a mid-table league team, they will have won around 37 per cent of their games, drawn 27 per cent, and lost the remainder. Winning is nowhere near three times harder than drawing, as is implied in the awarding of points. The result of this is that if you examine a team's record in terms of their league position or current form, using the three-one-nought points system, you end up with a very distorted view.

For this reason alone it is best not to put too much weight on any assessment of a team's performance that is based on points. Allowing for the home/away balance, there are six different match results we have to consider - the three possible ways that a game can end for both home and away matches. If you try to fit them along a scale from best to worst, all sorts of inconsistencies start to appear. A home draw is definitely worse than an away draw but a team picks up one point in both cases.

A win away is nearly twice as difficult to achieve as one at home, but both results are awarded the same three points. Goals are not an artificial measure, and as such should allow us to gauge the relative strength of teams more accurately. There is an average of just over 2.5 of them in any league game, with the home team managing about 1.5 per game and the away team 1.0.

Within this tally is a handy measure - the difference between the two is 0.5 of a goal. In spread betting terminology this is the average supremacy enjoyed by a home team. Expressing a team's capabilities in terms of the number of goals they score home and away is probably a far more reliable method of assessing performance than their points tally. The following current form table should illustrate this.

| Derby | | Aston Villa | |
|---|---|---|---|
| Last four games | | Last four games | |
| Home draw | 1-1 | Away loss | 0-1 |
| Away win | 1-0 | Home draw | 0-0 |
| Home draw | 1-1 | Away draw | 2-2 |
| Away loss | 1-3 | Away draw | 1-1 |

The tally of points in these four games reads Derby five, Aston Villa three. So there doesn't seem to be much problem in concluding that Derby have better current form. But if you look at how the teams performed compared to their expected home/away supremacies, things look very different.

Derby should have had a natural home supremacy of 0.5 of a goal when they went into their first game. But they only achieved a draw; effectively, a 'head start' was wiped out by their opponents, so we can say that Derby were actually 0.5 of a goal behind where they should have been.

When they won away by one goal they achieved a supremacy of 1.0, but started the game with a 0.5 goal deficit as the away side, so we can say they actually achieved a supremacy of 1.5 goals in this game.

Using the same system to assess all eight games, we discover that Derby, although scoring more points than Aston Villa, only achieved an overall supremacy of minus 1.0 goal (worse than the average team). Villa, despite only picking up three points in four games, have an overall supremacy of 0.0. So we might conclude that they are actually playing better than Derby.

Of course, we haven't taken into account the relative strengths of the opposition or any other factors, but the example illustrates how different assessment methods can radically alter our view of a team.

Using goals as a measure inevitably has some drawbacks. Goals are not necessarily equal in their importance. If a team is cruising along 3-0 up at home, the next goal in the game is not of vital importance. The home side might relax a bit and let one in towards the end of the game or manage one more themselves on the stroke of full-time. But a goal where the teams are locking horns at 1-1 is comparatively vital.

## betting on goals and correct scores

In terms of betting on the score of the game, the fixed-odds firms are little more than useless. Correct score bets are used as a bait to lure punters into longer-odds bets that seem more palatable than the skinny looking odds for the overall result.

If Spurs are 8-15 to win at home, 2-0 appears to be a reasonable forecast - and, at odds of 6-1, tempting to the unwary. But it is all a horrible illusion. The potential number of scorelines between two teams is higher than the man in the street might guess off the top of his head. In games with up to six goals, there are 28 combinations in which they can fall between the two teams - although some are far more likely than others.

With just one or two honourable exceptions, the margin built into correct score bets is so vast (Ladbrokes bet to a hideous 142 per cent on all scorelines containing six goals and under) that there can be virtually nothing ever to recommend about correct score betting. The odd way in which correct score prices are generated just occasionally throws up some discrepancies. Flip over a football coupon and the prices are presented as a table according to the odds on the home team. For some strange reason there are now two different odds tables.

In 1996, the leading firms decided there were not enough goals in European games to be able to use the usual tables. A home team rated at 4-5 to win is priced up at 6-1 on the domestic score chart - whereas for a side in a European competition or international match, similarly at 4-5, the odds for the 1-0 win shrink to 5-1. This apparently reflects the fact that domestic games have more goals. This may have been the case in the past but it certainly isn't now. The imposition of two different sets of prices throws up some stark discrepancies. Stanley Racing clearly states that its domestic score charts also applies to Italian Serie A games. The Italian Premiership contains fewer goals than just about any other grouping of games you can imagine, but Stanley lump the games into the table they reserve for competitions with a slightly higher number of goals.

In contrast, the 'international' list applies to the very low scoring games or the finals of major competitions like the World Cup and European Championship, but also applies to relatively uncompetitive friendlies that tend to contain a comparatively high number of goals.

The margins are so huge that the fixed-odds firms don't need to worry too much about minor lapses - although there is one scoreline where even the margins can't save them. Some years ago a few clued up people realised that 3-3 draws occurred in British football somewhat more than the odds of 100-1 implied. A swift clean up followed, causing odds to contract to 50-1.

With the perception that international and European competitions contained fewer goals, many firms, including Ladbrokes, left their European 3-3 odds at 100-1. The likelihood of a 3-3 draw in matches covered by the international 'correct score' chart is about the same as in the UK, about one in 65; 100-1 for a European 3-3 is the one example of a correct score where there is a theoretical profit in favour of the backer.

The number of goals occurring in a game can be wagered on the spread companies' 'total goals' market and the fixed-odds' equivalent markets. On the fixed-odds, the main firms have bottled out of this sort of betting by offering three price brackets. Hills generally go 2-1 for a game to contain fewer than two goals, 5-2 for exactly two goals, and 4-5 more than two.

There tends to be a fundamental bias within all goals betting reflecting that the only thing people want to do is back a game to contain plenty of goals. This is so prevalent that for live TV games it is impossible for the spread firms to attract equal money either side of the spread. If the game contains fewer than three goals they tend to win overall, whatever the actual result. If more than five goals appear they almost always lose heavily.

There is plenty of evidence that you should never be high on goals. Looking at the actual frequencies of the brackets against Hills' odds reveal that they take a huge margin from those who want to back goals. They generally offer 4-6 (60 per cent) in the 'over three goals' bracket, when fewer than 50 per cent of games actually fall into this category.

The margin is at its smallest in the 'exactly two goals' bracket - 2-1, an implied percentage of 33.3, whereas the true frequency is 27 per cent. The margin in the low-bracket is slightly higher than the mid-bracket. Even on the spreads the quotes seem naturally to favour sellers. The average midpoint of a quote appears to be 2.63, slightly above the true frequency of goals per game.

To punish clients for their consistent goal-buying behaviour, the spread companies make sure they take a bit more margin from them than they would on any other trade. The implication of this is that there is probably little to be gained by developing a superb model for predicting games with a high number of goals, as there is no fair way to bet on them.

# chapter **eleven**

# **corners**

Whenever a piece appears in the national press on the joys of spread betting, the journalist frequently expresses astonishment at the fact that anyone could be remotely interested in gambling on the number of corners in a football match. In fact, there are good reasons for why this spread market and equivalent fixed-odds bets (with Stan James, William Hill and Coral) are prime punting territory. On a fairly basic level, it is a satisfyingly exciting bet. Corners appear every eight minutes or so, and the range of conceivable make-ups (between three and 24 for a single game) is large enough to be more attractive than the relatively skimpy number of goals. But it's not so vast as the potentially wallet-bashing volatility of, for example, 'time of the first goal'.

A particularly attractive aspect of corner betting is that it exists in a sort of parallel universe from the strength of the teams. If it were simply the case that the best teams won loads of corners, and the worst very few, then the corner count would simply be a more heavily geared version of a standard 'goals supremacy' bet. As such it would be easy to price, and therefore difficult to beat. In fact there are a host of factors effecting a team's ability to win corners that are quite separate from their overall league rating. A team miles out in front at the top of the division may well spend more time in their opponent's half than other sides, and they'll probably have more shots on goal than anyone else. But they won't necessarily win the most corners or be involved in a disproportionate number of games in which the corner count is high.

The corner count revolves around a number of tactical considerations. As such it is perhaps the perfect betting medium for footballing superbrains.

Anyone with an in-depth knowledge of particular team's style of play is in a particularly advantageous position - which is seldom the case when it comes to actual match betting.

The situations that lead to corners aren't as clear cut as some might imagine. The scenario that instantly springs to mind is where a goalkeeper tips a shot around the post. TV programmes frequently dust off the footage of England's disastrous night against Poland at Wembley in 1973. Watching Poland's goalkeeper, Jan Tomasheszi, over 25 years later, demonstrates one aspect of how the game has evolved. On that night Tomasheszi put paid to England's chances of World Cup Finals qualification with a series of spectacular, if over dramatised saves, almost all of which went out for corners. In the intervening years, goalkeeping has become something of an all-or-nothing skill.

Either keepers save and hold onto the ball, or it finds its way into the net. In the last few years the art of tipping the ball over the bar has virtually become redundant. British league goalkeepers tend to be so tall they can catch a ball at any height which risks going into the goal, or alternatively simply let it sail over.

So the role of goalkeepers in giving away corners has become diminished. This in turn means that shots on target are not necessarily closely related to corners. The key to the number of corners is actually to look at what is happening on the wings. In an attack down the right-hand side, what is the one situation that is the most favourable if you want a high number of corners?

Strangely, what you can probably do without is the ball to find its way into the penalty-area. If the person on the ball is David Beckham, that is where it is likely to end up, as he is particularly adept at crossing the ball from deep positions. What you really need is a player to dash towards the opponent's goal-line and try to cross the ball in. Where a defender shadows an attacker who tries to go to the outside, the chances of a corner in the next few seconds are probably higher than in any other tactical situation. Either the attacker manages to whip the ball across or the defender flings a leg in to divert the ball, invariably for a corner.

But what happens to the chances of a corner if the attacking player cuts inside the defender? At the moment the attacker cuts inside, the buyer of corners can safely chuck something at the TV. In this case the chance of a corner resulting immediately plummets. This illustrates a key tactical point. The best set-up for corner buyers is where a team plays two out-and-out wingers. It helps enormously if the left winger has a suspect right foot (and the right winger a non-existent left foot) as they will tend to force themselves into the corners to deliver crosses. It also makes a difference as to what type of player is waiting for crosses.

In general, beefy English-style centre-forwards are slightly better for getting into corner-inducing situations, as they rely on a significant 'havoc' factor.

Since they are slightly happier to have the ball delivered high and muscle in on goal, there is a greater chance of defenders getting something in the way or challenging for a header. A gang of diminutive continentals, playing the ball to each other's feet is slightly worse for corners, as they tend either to pass the ball into the net or get clattered head-on by a bruiser of a central defender.

Corners have a tendency to lead to more corners. You will probably recall situations where they suddenly appear in a flurry of three or four. This tends, again, to happen because of a 'chaos factor' in the penalty-area. Certain types of corner-takers are more prone to produce another corner immediately. Any player who whips the ball in - i.e. where it is very fast, follows a fairly flat trajectory and bends in towards goal - is a gem for producing another corner quickly. Takers who let it drift long, at a high trajectory, are not so good. Sides who take short corners are, in general, the worst of the lot. The moment the corner-taker passes back, away from the goal-line, the defenders tend to push out slightly and face towards the centre-circle, meaning that if they can intercept the cross it is more likely to go firmly away from goal.

The key oddity with the corners market is the problems that occur when trying to pinpoint the 'average' number of corners in a game. This is not just of theoretical interest; it is a difficulty that bookmakers appear to have significant problems with, to the extent that there are opportunities for punters to take advantage of.

The key to the genuine pricing errors which occur is that there are three different measures of central tendency - what we tend to lump together and call the 'average'. Although it could apply to all three, the *average* of a range of values is generally understood to be the 'arithmetic mean' - in the case of corners, the number that have been awarded divided by the number of games in which they appeared in. In fact the number of corners in a season fluctuates significantly, but at present stands at around 11.3 per game.

This figure of 11.3, though statistically correct, doesn't quite present a totally reliable estimate of how many corners we should expect in a game. In fact the starkest illustration of how problems with averages can throw up unexpected answers appears whenever there is a discussion of 'average' earnings. Whenever the Government releases the figures for how much we are calculated to earn, a lot of people suddenly feel hard done by.

Imagine a group of 200 people, each earning £16,000 a year. Their total earnings are £3.2m; clearly, dividing this figure by the number of people (200) gets us back to an arithmetic mean of £16,000. But creeping in unannounced is a Premiership footballer who earns a cool £2m per year. There are now 201 members of the group earning a total of £5.2 million. The makes the group's average earnings £25,870 per year. When told this figure, there are not surprisingly gasps of astonishment. Two hundred people feel very poor as they realise they are earning well below the average figure. The footballer keeps quiet. It is his relatively astronomical wages that have tugged the arithmetic mean to a completely misleading figure.

To give a more accurate reflection of how much the country earns it is better to use a completely different measure of central tendency, the median. If all the values were laid out in order of lowest to highest, the median is the value that lies exactly halfway. In the earnings example, this would be one of the figures of £16,000 - a figure that gives a better impression of earnings then the arithmetic mean, which has been corrupted by the one freak figure of the footballer.

The number of corners in each match are similarly affected, though not quite so dramatically. The mean is just over 11, but more match tallies finish below this figure than above it. In the same way as earnings, there is a fixed point at which the number of corners in a game can't sink below (zero), but there is a tiny chance of a huge number of corners appearing - 24 being the largest make-up in the most recent Premiership season. There is no chance of a game finishing in 12 corners less than the mean, but it is possible that it can finish 12 corners above the mean.

In terms of spread betting this doesn't matter. So long as the mid-point of the quote is firmly anchored around the arithmetic mean, then is must be correct. Sellers win slightly more often but slightly less in hard cash than buyers. The latter have to wait slightly longer for wins, but when they materialise that have the potential to be larger than that of sellers. Pricing errors can creep in when a fixed-odds firm offers prices based on a spread company's quotes.

Going back to the earnings example for a moment, imagine that a fixed-odds company wanted to offer prices based on the arithmetic mean of people's annual wages. They see that the mean is over £25,000 for our sample, and innocently offer 10-11 that a person's earnings will be less than £25,500 and 10-11 that they will be over £25,000. In this situation you would clearly want to lump on the 'under' bracket. They are estimating there is around a 50 per cent chance that someone earns lower than the mean, when the sample reveals that 200 in 201 people actually do.

This fundamental error appears to creep into some betting markets, including corners. The basic advice to stem from this is that you should never back a high number of corners in a game at fixed-odds prices. Hills generally offer 6-5 for a game to result in more than 12 corners. Don't be tempted. The actual percentage of games finishing in 13 corners or more is a measly 36 per cent. The consequence is that Hills can take very little money from backers of the other two prices brackets: 2-1 is offered on a game containing fewer than 10 corners and also the middle bracket of 10-12 corners. Here, the true percentages, 32 per cent for both low and medium number of corners, are only a shade lower than those implied in the odds (33 per cent).

Stan James are very keen to offer bets based on spread markets. Until midway through the 2000-2001 season, they offered Evens on a game to result in fewer than 12 corners. This was not an accurate reflection of the actual distribution. Around 55 per cent of games result in fewer than 12 corners, so there was a huge opportunity to be had in going low with them. More recently they have adjusted their price brackets so that they now go Evens for fewer than 11 corners, bringing them back within the realms of mathematical safety.

Whatever the statistical basis for the market, both the fixed-odds companies and the spread firms only see significant business on the high side. Sellers of corners are in the minority. As a result there is sometimes talk of the market being permanently better for sellers. This is certainly true on the fixed-odds, but the position on the spreads is marginal. Over time the quotes might be set at about 0.3 greater than the true frequency of corners, leading to the conclusion that, whatever the circumstances, going high on corners is inadvisable. In some ways this is unfortunate, as the tactical pointers to a game with high corners are fairly clear.

For the corner buyers there is no more enticing market than multi-corners, the spread firms' more heavily geared version of the standard corners market. Here, first-half corners are multiplied by second-half corners to produce the make-up. This creates another mathematical illusion that is easy to trip over. In a game with 12 corners, it is possible to imagine the make-up must be 36 (6 x 6). This is actually the maximum possible make-up. It is theoretically possible that the corners could split 12 in the first-half and none in the second, leaving a make-up of zero (12 x 0).

Taking a weighted average of all the possible first/second-half splits reveals that the best estimate of the make-up in a game containing 12 corners is 33, three fewer than the maximum. The fact that the arithmetic mean of corners per game is somewhat under 12 leaves the mean multi-corner make-up at 32.5, bang in the middle of spread quotes - these range from 27-30 to 34-37. If you must buy corners, then the multi-corner market is possibly the one to go for as it doesn't appear naturally to benefit sellers as much as the fixed-odds and standard spread quotes.

The one situation in which buying may be a sound policy is where one team is overwhelmingly superior, though such games almost never appear in the British leagues. Where international minnows such as Andorra and San Marino take the stage there are inevitably huge supremacy quotes in favour of their opponents. In general the corners quote for such games only rises to 12-13 (greater than the usual quotes of 10.5-11.5 and 11-12).

My experience is that this doesn't reflect the fact teams that are really up against it have a rather different attitude to giving away corners. They are liable to see them as a small victory - i.e. the ball didn't go in the goal - rather than something to be avoided at all costs. As a result the corner count tends to be higher than the bookies' estimations in these circumstances.

Trading in-running may be one of the advantages of spread betting, but recently it has been of little use in the corners market. The firms open their quotes with a one-point spread but do not appear to narrow this as the game progresses. As a result, once you've traded this market you are just about stuck with it. If, with 15 minutes to go, you want to close a trade, the full one point spread can be the equivalent of 20 per cent of the possible make-ups. In spread betting terms this is a very large margin, and one at which it is certainly best not to trade on in all but the most desperate circumstances.

Spread firms now offer a corners supremacy market, using the same principle as goals supremacy. Therefore, Arsenal/Ipswich might attract a quote of 2-3, suggesting that Arsenal will win 2-3 corners more than Ipswich. The ability to back a particular side is a useful innovation, as previously both teams' corner count had to be considered when playing the 'total corners' market.

The corner supremacy quote is primarily based on a team's goal supremacy quote. After all, a team scoring more goals should also win more corners. But any indication that a side's corner-winning ability is out of line with its general strength is worth seizing upon. So a key pattern is when a strong side, with a relatively poor recent corner record, is up against a basically poor team, one better than its league position suggests, who have an ability to gain corners. In this situation, you should look to back the poorer team, as the corner supremacy quote may be too anchored to the overall goal supremacy line.

chapter **twelve**

# bookings

Considering referees have to put up constant barracking from crowds questioning their impartiality, it says a lot for their unbending professionalism that there has never been any hint of funny goings-on in the bookings market. The scale of spread trading on bookings is phenomenal (lying third to supremacy and total goals trading) as it has only a passing relevance to the game of football itself. One day, sooner or later, questions are going to be asked about the integrity of a market that is solely based on one man's decisions about the behaviour of the players, rather than their actual competitive endeavours. But for now, the bookings market is a fascinating challenge as the make-up of a game is such an intriguing brew of different factors.

The 25 points for a red card and 10 points for a yellow card is now the accepted way of framing both spread quotes and the fixed-odds. It shares the same attributes as the corners and total goals market of being markedly skewed. The average Premiership make-up in 2000-2001 was 35.6, but only 161 out of 380 games (42.4 per cent) resulted in make-ups above this mean. The conceivable make-ups are between zero and 120, meaning that the downside for buyers is much less than the upside - so, again in common with the corners and total corners market, buyers of bookings far outnumber sellers.

There are a few hard figures released from the spread companies that bear out this. For seven games played on 31 February 2001, City Index, now trading as Blue Square for sports betting, announced a loss of £12,000 on the market where the average make-up over seven games was 51. Their biggest losses are where there are very high make-ups in live TV games.

As with just about all football stats, bookings are subject to a fundamental home/away imbalance. The mean make-up per team is about 16 for home sides, but 20 for away sides. This has echoes of a statistic about penalties - that home teams are much more likely to be awarded them than the away side. There is sometimes talk of this being due to the fact the referee is pressured by the home crowd into awarding penalties, but there is likely to be a more down to earth explanation.

Since home teams have a natural supremacy, they tend to get the ball into the visitor's penalty-area more often than vice-versa, so they legitimately win more penalties. The same can probably be said for the fact that the poor visitors have more players booked. Since, on average, they spend a far greater period of the match losing than their opponents, it is no wonder they are slightly more hot-tempered.

One of the great spread betting talking points of recent times was BBC2's excellent *Jackpot* series, which featured a chap named Philip who reportedly won £500,000 by targeting certain matches and selling the bookings market. This had me diving headlong into the stats to try to fathom out how this feat was possible. There is no evidence this market is structurally set too high, though it was clear he was selling in games where there appeared to be a subjective chance of a very high make-up.

This brings us to the core of the market - the relationship between the previous disciplinary records of the teams and the previous record of the official. The degree of variation in both is considerable. Season means for referees vary between 22 for the most lenient official and 55 for the strictest. The most undisciplined team tends to earn around 23 points per game, with the best behaved coming in at slightly less than 10. From this it would appear relatively easy to arrive at an accurate assessment of the make-up for a single match. Construct a formula that weights the three factors (home side's disciplinary record, away side's record, and referee's record; shift the whole thing around a bit to take into account the home/away imbalance - and you should end up with a good estimate).

As ever, it's not that simple (which is probably just as well as it would be too easy for a company to churn out mathematically-perfect quotes). The first problem comes back to the use of averages (yet again). Just looking at the records of the teams it is clear there is a distinction to be made between 'aggro' matches and 'calm' matches. Throughout the season most teams face traditional rivals, often local derbies, but also clashes where there is some historical bad blood, for example Arsenal v Leeds. The trouble with using a blanket average to describe a team's disciplinary record is that it mixes the explosive games with the routine one, whereas there is a case for saying that the two are so distinct they should be considered separately.

By lumping them all in together, it is like trying to forecast how many goals England will score against Holland on the basis of figures which include their goal tally against San Marino. You are effectively trying to compare two very different variables.

The top clubs have a tendency to get involved in rough matches with other leading contenders, but have relatively quiet affairs against lesser teams. In general, the sparks fly where there is a combination of Manchester United, Leeds, Arsenal, Chelsea and Liverpool. In 2000-2001, there were 40 games between these clubs, producing an average make-up of 51 per game, massively above the overall average of 35.6. But without these 40 bad-tempered affairs the figure of 35.6 is meaningless. If you get rid of just the 40 key games from the sample the average of the remainder drops to 32.8.

This can be taken further by separating the obvious needle of local derbies to establish two quite separate and distinct averages, where it is fairly easy in advance to slot any individual game into one of the two categories - aggro or calm games. The effect of this is that there are two baseline figures running through the Premier League. When you try to mix them up, it is easy to draw the wrong conclusion about a game that is about to take place.

If Leeds face Southampton, their raw disciplinary record contains information taken from games where there was an identifiable aggro factor. But against the Saints this simply doesn't exist. A fairer assessment of Leeds' potential for bookings in this game is to look at their record in calm matches and largely ignore their obviously highly-charged encounters.

If the previous records of clubs are coloured by a mean that is based on somewhat irrelevant information, then there must be an implication for betting on bookings. If, in the Leeds game, they bring some bogus statistical baggage with them, suggesting they are a comparatively rough team, then the bookings quote on the match may be slightly higher than strictly necessary.

The reverse must also be true. Teams involved in a needle match bring averages to the game which are based on the results of their calm matches, so you might expect the quote to be marginally too low. The companies offering quotes are therefore in a statistical straightjacket, hovering too close to the overall mean of around 35.

Having compared quotes to make-ups, I'd tentatively suggest this might be the case. My advice is to look to trade *with* the quote. So if the quote is low - e.g. 27-32, think in terms of going lower. If it is high - e.g. 37-41 - consider buying. I reckon that using this technique alone could be enough to secure a profit of about 40 points in every 100 trades; not a spectacular return, but one that could be improved considerably by looking at other factors.

Having said there might be an advantage in buying high quotes, I would never admit doing so. To do it puts us in exactly the same position as the hordes of buyers who see a violent encounter on the cards and buy in the hope of a few cheap thrills. Following the crowd and betting with the vast majority of account holders doesn't appeal, so the advice should probably be trimmed to 'when low, go lower'.

After the *Jackpot* programme, I became convinced that Philips' winnings must have been earned by using previous game stats in an unexpected way. Trying to pick up as many clues as possible from the content of the programme, I noticed he seemed to be concentrating more on the record and motivation of the referees than the teams. The previous games' make-ups in which a referee has officiated are widely known.

My first line of inquiry was whether he was turning this information on its head. I read David Elleray's biography in an attempt to pick up clues as to how the top referees look at their job. It was clear they are somewhat more concerned at having a good game, in which their decisions were both technically correct and fair, than may generally be appreciated amongst the ref-baiting public as a whole.

Particularly bad-tempered games appear to concern Elleray greatly and the risk of being taken to task by his assessors is a constant headache. In an interesting account of how fraught the life of a top official can be, he countered the view that referees ever enjoyed being confrontational. I wondered whether it was possible that, following a particularly heated encounter, the referee might go to the next game in a relatively forgiving frame of mind, hoping to avoid successive high card counts.

Premiership referees also take charge of lower division and cup games, so trying to piece together all the information for analysis is a huge task, but I wouldn't be surprised if there is a tendency for referees to follow a very high make-up game with a comparatively low one.

There is also the intriguing possibility that the same thing applies to the sides themselves, or at least individual players. Having got booked in the preceding game, there must be a chance that players are keen to avoid successive cautions.

The stats appear to demonstrate this might be the case. Where a team has had four players or more booked in the game before, it seems to behave slightly better than its own average in the next game. In addition, teams involved in high profile needle matches, particularly derbies, may experience a drop in aggression factor for the game immediately afterwards.

There is a slight difficulty in assessing the make-ups of a referee's previous game. Graham Barber appears, on paper, to be the strictest official in the Premiership (his average make-up for 2000-01 was 50). On the other hand, Paul Durkin looks relatively lenient, with an average of just 22. This would seem to suggest that if the same dubious challenge was played out in front of both of them, Barber would be more likely to award a card than Durkin.

But a look not just at the two officials' previous make-ups, but also which teams were playing reveals that we are not comparing like with like. Graham Barber got lumbered with a disproportionate number of potentially aggro-filled matches, including Chelsea v West Ham, Arsenal v Manchester United, Leeds v Manchester United, and Newcastle v Middlesbrough. The less experienced referees are booked in for the less nasty looking games.

I wouldn't dare to claim, on the basis of this, that all referees are the same. Graham Barber is clearly stricter in calm looking games than other referees are. However, I wonder whether the degree of difference in the criteria they apply for handing out bookings is slightly less than the spreads account for. If this is the case, then there might be an advantage in giving the teams' previous records somewhat more weight than that of the official. One exception to the 'trade with the quote rule' might be where a strict referee is in charge of a quiet looking game.

Inevitably, the bookings market structurally favours sellers, since there are so many eager to buy. The margins built into the buy side are much greater than that of the sell side, to the extent that consistent sellers are unlikely to lose much, if anything. It is clear that the bookings market can be a paradoxical affair. Dirty teams might suddenly become clean ones, strict referees might not be as strict as they seem and peace-loving teams might explode into a frenzy when they meet their hated rivals. It is a market where the stats have to be used very carefully, because first impressions, as ever, can often lead to the wrong conclusion.

chapter **thirteen**

# **fair, rain or shine**

As I write, I am constantly sneaking a look out of the window at the thickening grey skies. Tomorrow sees the start of both a cricket Test match and the British Open Golf Championship. There is hardly any betting aspect of the two events that isn't weather related - how many runs will be scored, how many players will achieve an under-par score, which players will respond to the conditions best. I can dream that sticking my head out of the front door will give me an advantage over the bookies, but of course they are quite capable of getting the weather forecast off teletext and adjusting prices accordingly. For a huge variety of sports the weather is a key factor, but in football it is almost totally neglected.

In terms of beating the odds, football punters have a decisive advantage when it comes to the weather. Because the odds in the shops are released a few days in advance, we know there is no possibility they will have been framed with meteorology in mind. On the face of it weather might seem only to have the most marginal effect on the result of a football match, but my research suggests that some bookies, particularly those who offer odds on the number of goals in each game, might be extremely vulnerable to weather-related bets.

My largest ever accumulative win was with Stanley Racing (seven out of eight selections correct) on the basis of nothing more than it being a very windy day. What makes the weather such a potent factor is the fact that it provides a common relating factor between a number of games. This is explored in detail in chapter fifteen.

The general subject of weather can be lumped together with a discussion on the state of pitches to form a broad category of 'conditions'. The subject often rears its head when a Premiership outfit has to play a lower league team away in the FA Cup. The usual scenario is that someone like Arsenal have to play non-league Lymeswold away in the third round. Lymeswold's pitch isn't up to much - a cratered mudscape not really suited to football. Arsenal's manager starts moaning that the match venue should be switched. The cry goes up from their humble opponents, the press and everyone else, "It's the same for both sides!"

Of course they are correct, but actually Arsenal are probably right to complain. The problem they face is that they have an in-built supremacy over Lymeswold of probably more than three goals per game, *if* the match is played in normal conditions. But in this case, it isn't. The more factors that are introduced that make the match less like a normal football game, the more disadvantaged the favourites (the ones with natural superiority) become.

To illustrate this, we can introduce a quite drastic change to the game to see what effect it would have on the odds. In a normal game, played at a neutral venue, Lymeswold might attract a quote of 18-1. But unfortunately, due to an administrative oversight, there are no footballs available at kick-off. It is decided that the game must take place anyway (to avoid fixture congestion), so someone manages to produce a rugby ball to use instead.

At this point in the ridiculous scenario, what should Lymeswold's odds be? They should probably be equally rated with Arsenal. The fact that the Premiership high-flyers have to play with an oval rugby ball has just nullified their entire natural supremacy. As everyone dashes around the field after a ball bobbling eccentrically in all directions, most of the skills that they are better than Lymeswold at - tackling, dribbling, moving into space, etc - suddenly count for nothing.

This absurd example should illustrate a key point. The less like 'normal' football a game becomes, the greater the chance of a team who are basically inferior. The weather is one factor that can significantly change the balance of natural superiority. This tends to be generally acknowledged but not acted upon. It is common to hear pundits talk of icy, snowy or otherwise atrocious playing conditions to cause surprising results. The advice tends to follow, "Don't bet for a while - sit it out until form settles down again."

In fact the settling down of form is usually the last thing we want. The imposition of odd factors on the results of football matches is in our favour as it damages the odds compilers' serene ability to use the usual formulae for pricing games. If the weather intervenes, you should be looking to oppose favourites. Snow particularly stunts the favourite's ability to assert their natural supremacy.

There aren't that many examples of British teams suffering white-outs internationally, though notably in late October 1997, Chelsea were forced to play Tromso, in the arctic conditions of northern Norway, taking with them a supremacy spread of 1.4 -1.7. Dark 24 hours a day in winter, a trip to staggeringly cold Tromso tends to be something people don't forget in a hurry. Chelsea lost 3-2, though they managed to repair the damage with a ridiculously easy 7-1 win back in London, the scale of their superiority in their home-leg going to show how the Norwegian climate had got to them.

On a point of academic interest, Sporting Index is said to have suffered their biggest-ever loss on a single football match having posted a supremacy quote of 1.3-1.6 for Chelsea in the return-leg.

Like a shower, if it's not too cold, it's too hot. After a period of acclimatisation, teams playing in conditions they might find alien perform reasonably well. The English national team, with a reasonable amount of time to adapt to conditions in Mexico, put in creditable performances in the World Cups of 1970 and 1986, considering the vast problems of playing up a mountain in seething temperatures. But without much preparation teams wilt alarmingly. Manchester United were a shadow of their usual selves when controversially entered into a South American tournament in the middle of the 1999-2000 season.

Horrible British weather hits in a variety of guises. I have some slender evidence that different conditions effect the result in different ways. Aside from the actual result, the variable that needs close attention is the number of goals in a game under varying conditions. I have recorded the general conditions alongside the results of matches for a couple of seasons and seem to have found a semblance of a pattern.

Very wet, cut-up pitches appear to be bad for goals. The difference between a completely drenched pitch and a normal one possibly accounts for around 0.6 of a goal per game. Subjectively there are reasons for this. On a wet pitch the ball travels slightly slower than normal and cannot run as far. As in the rugby ball example, it can help deliberately to imagine an extreme set of conditions.

This time try to imagine the effects of playing with a very heavy medicine ball that it is almost impossible to get moving. The game would degenerate into a shoving match between the two sides as they endured an ungainly struggle to advance a few feet. In these circumstances it is very unlikely that it would be possible to score at all.

This seems to contradict the often held view that damp conditions make it uniquely difficult for defenders. My reading of the stats is that the opposite might be the case. Defenders may find the ball slightly easier to keep track of when wet. I tend to go against the other common view about the weather as well - that very windy conditions are bad for goals. According to my records, wind actually contributes to the goal tally to the extent that we can expect around 0.4 more goals per game if there is a roaring gale. If a wet, heavy ball contributes to few goals being scored, then perhaps hot, sunny conditions aid goals slightly. My records seem to show this is the case.

This fact could underlie the general pattern of a high goal count during the first few weeks of the season (in August and September), tailing off towards December and January, only to take an upturn towards the end of the season in April. As will become clear in the chapter on related bets, any weekend where all the matches show similar 'goal properties' can be highly significant from a betting point of view.

The first round of matches in 2001-2002 was held particularly early in Scotland - the Scottish Premiership kicked off on 28 July 2001. This particular day was one of the hottest in the UK in recent years and I was not surprised that three or more goals occurred in all six games taking place that day, an occurrence that would only be expected in a group of six games in one out of every 100 times.

chapter **fourteen**

# a new view on singles

If I had entitled this chapter 'How to get a single on all matches' a lot of readers might have been entitled to switch off immediately, having thought they'd heard this all before. What I am not proposing is to describe the time-honoured way of achieving a single bet on a league game - the half-time/full-time forecast. There are two alternative ways of achieving a 'single' - both mathematically better than half-time/full-time forecasts, though which you choose is a matter of how sure you are about your main selection.

At the time of writing, the rule regarding the acceptance of singles is murky. By offering singles on all Premiership games, Surrey Sports, the Tote, Blue Square and Bet Direct have defied the long standing FA ruling that single bets cannot be accepted on non-live British games. The FA appears reluctantly to concede that it can't control the offering of singles by companies operating outside Britain, but seeing as a lot of off-shore firms may be returning to Britain, the picture remains unclear.

In the meantime, I believe the technically best way to get a single is as follows: Let's say you are convinced that Cardiff City are going to win at Macclesfield on Saturday afternoon. No bookie will accept a bet on Cardiff City unless it is either paired with a selection in a live TV game, or combined in a treble with two other draw or away win predictions. The problem with backing all the combinations of half-time/full-time forecasts is that all the companies build a large margin into the odds - the over-round is about 125 per cent generally.

We'll say that it is Hills who are offering the best price on Cardiff of 11-4. The trick is to pair this in a double with any selection from a live game that takes place *after* your main selection where Hills are offering the best price. There might be a choice of three live games on the coupon. With two of them Hills are not offering a best price on any of the three possible results, but in a Scottish match between Hibs and Motherwell (to be televised on Sunday afternoon), they go best-priced 6-5 for Hibs. It doesn't matter what views, if any, you have on the Scottish match - it is simply important that you back just one of the results in a double with your primary bet.

If Cardiff are not victorious, then the double falls - but at least unlike using half-time/full-time forecasts, you haven't had the hassle of placing loads of bets. Should Cardiff win you now have the winnings from the Cardiff match running on to Hibs. If your stake was £50 on the double, £187.50 is running on Hibs the next day. In the event of a Hibs victory the return is £412.50.

It is now just a question of hedging on the other two results, the draw and a Motherwell away victory, to ensure you make an automatic profit across the whole bet. The nifty part of this is that, as singles are now allowed on the live game you have the opportunity of hedging at the best prices. It might be that Coral are best-priced on the draw at 12-5 and Stan James best for the away win, at 5-2, adding up to an overall best-price percentage of 103.4 per cent.

To achieve correct proportional staking for the hedge on the draw, you need to press the following buttons on the calculator, 412.50 multiplied by 29.41 per cent. The 412.50 is the total we'll win if the first double comes off: 29.41 is the percentage associated with the odds of 12-5. The answer should be £121.31. Get rid of the odd £1.21, which will irritate the bookie, and the stake on the draw should be £120.

Similarly, the stake on the away win is 412.50 multiplied by 28.57 per cent (the figure of 28.57 is the associated percentage of the odds 5-2). This comes to 117.85 - or again more likely in practice to be £120.

Having hedged the other two results, we're not that bothered about the score in the Scottish game. Whatever happens we will win a little over £400. I won't bore you too much with the proof that the margin in the bookies' favour on this bet is less than that in half-time/full-time forecasts, but a calculation of the win/lose ratios should confirm that it is considerably less than 125 per cent.

Strictly speaking, it could be argued that the best way of backing a 'single' match is to double it with a very strong home favourite in a live game, and not bother to hedge at all. The proviso is that the odds-on 'certainty' should be best-priced - or at least very close to best-priced - with the same company who are best-priced on your main selection.

This tactic is quite commonly pursued. Even though there is a chance of the double going down when the good thing fails, we know there is very little margin built into the prices of heavily odds-on favourites. Therefore one double at a very low margin in favour of the bookie is superior to one low margin double plus two single bets on higher margin draws and, especially, away wins.

chapter **fifteen**

# related and semi-independent bets

At some time in our punting lives most of us will have indulged in sending off for information from one of those small ads claiming to show us 'the way to win a fortune from betting'. What came back was invariably some mad staking system or similarly hopeless plan designed to fleece the terminally naive. But if you can cast cynicism aside for a few moments, there is, I believe, one type of multiple bet that, to anyone prepared to be reasonably patient, offers the promise of stacking up a huge accumulator win for small stakes. But the opportunity doesn't come without needing a bit of brainpower to apply to one of the most obscure and difficult areas that football betting throws up.

The basis is the area of related bets and the possibility that when single bets at the correct odds are put into a multiple bet (doubles, trebles and upwards), the odds on the multiple bet mysteriously turn in our favour. It is a non-sporting example of this principle in action that probably provides the best example.

Say the weather forecast predicts a day of mixed weather, with a 50 per cent chance of rain. If a bookie was to offer odds on something that was predicted a 50 per cent chance, he might offer odds of 5-6. Along the same lines there is about a 50 per cent chance that, at some point in the day, you see somebody that is holding an umbrella. In bookies terms this is also a 5-6 chance. You will have to humour me for a moment for suggesting that a bookie might offer odds on this sort of thing. Both sets of odds are technically correct as they represent percentages slightly greater than the estimate of the true chances.

But see what happens when we try to place a double. A £10 double on it raining tomorrow (5-6) and seeing someone holding an umbrella (5-6) pays

£33.60p, accumulative odds of over 9-4. Are these odds a fair reflection of both events happening? It is fairly easy to see that they are not - if the Evens chance of it raining actually occurs then it is almost certain that we will see someone with an umbrella. Therefore the true chances of the double are about the same as the chances of the most fundamental single (that it will rain). So in this case we appear to be getting 9-4 on an eventuality that is, in reality, more like an Evens chance. The two elements of the double are obviously related.

At this point I should state that what I'm proposing in no way breaks the established bookmaker rules on the acceptance of related bets. It's simply that the rules as they stand cannot possibly cover a variety of situations where there could be a relationship between the legs of a multiple bet. Taking a close look at Ladbrokes' rules, the more blatant related bets are specifically disallowed, and if accepted in error the stake on the multiple bet is split into singles covering all the bet's elements.

Ladbrokes rules give the following as an example - a double on Manchester United to win 2-1, with Manchester United to win in 90 minutes. This is clearly unacceptable. The two outcomes are related to each other. If United win, a vast number of correct score possibilities are impossible.

Another often-cited example is also clear-cut. If Cole is 5-1 to score the first goal during Man United's match with Everton, you will not be allowed to place a double with Man United to win 1-0 at 6-1. The accumulative odds of 41-1 are an over-generous reflection of the chance of both events happening. One event is intricately bound up with the other. If Cole scores, one correct score possibility is instantly wiped out, that of the 0-0. A single event, the goal, has made it slightly more likely that you are going to pick up on two legs at accumulative odds.

The other situation where there is a degree of consensus is where one player or team is engaged in a number of different events. If Liverpool are 16-1 to win the FA Cup and 8-1 to win the League Championship, you probably won't be allowed a double. If they are good enough to win one event it suggests that the chances of them winning another are slightly enhanced. The act of doing well in the league is related to their ability to do well in the cup; therefore the events that make up the double are not completely independent.

There are a huge variety of situations where the rules are not clear and other examples where the rules as they stand do not even hint that some bets are dubious. Bookies rules on related bets tend to concentrate on areas where one event directly effects the outcome of another event. However, to my mind, for the accumulative odds to be 'fair' there must not be any possible hint of a relationship between the two legs. Not only must the legs be unrelated, but also a single factor must not influence the outcome of both results. It is the latter fact that bookies seem gloriously unaware of.

Where there is a relating factor this might be called a semi-independent bet. This occurs in a situation where there appears, on the face of it, to be no particular relationship between elements of a multiple bet - but in fact, lurking in the background, is a factor that is influencing the results of all the components. The elements are only semi-independent. For the bookie to be safe the elements must be totally independent.

I have just spotted a classic example of a semi-independent bet at the time of writing, though unfortunately not from a football market. Stan James are particularly prone to getting hammered on these types of wagers as they offer a variety of exotic bets on the same event that are liable to become inter-related. With some astonishment I came across a golf bet on their teletext page on the score of two players in their next round. You could bet that Bernhard Langer would score a round of over 70 at 2-1 and Padraig Harrington would also score over 70 at 2-1. Singles and doubles were accepted.

On the face of it there can be no link between the two. If Langer has a poor round, it doesn't make Harrington have a bad round as well. Even though the two elements are seemingly unrelated there is a bookie-bashing factor ready to strike - that of the weather. Calm, bright weather contributes to low scoring all round. Wet, windy conditions make low scoring almost impossible. The weather provides a key relating factor between the players scores.

Even the most cursory glance at the records of all competitors in a golf tournament reveals that something makes them all score well or all score poorly. Their scores in each the four rounds tend to bobble up and down in a huge tide of relatedness. If Langer scores a comparatively poor round compared to par, it is more likely that many other players will score poor rounds as well.

Here, a double on both players to score over 70 is tremendous value. But the fact that Stan James have allowed such a straightforward loophole indicates the general lack of appreciation of this principle. In football the effects of the weather are not quite as dramatic, but nevertheless are powerful enough to cause all sorts of problems with the odds on offer, and a number of opportunities for us.

It is quite common to find odds offered on a game to contain either 'more than two goals' (at odds of around 8-11) or 'less than three goals' (11-10). I know that at the end of the 2000-2001 season, the Tote chain of bookmakers were offering this low margin bet. Stanley Racing also offered a similar market on all

English and Scottish Premiership games but, rather meanly, towards the end of the season, split the bet into three brackets rather than two, instantly increasing the margin.

When Leeds United run out for a game in Yorkshire there seems no way that another Premiership match at, for example, West Ham can possibly be linked. The two matches appear totally separate, a bet on something happening at Leeds has no connection with a similar something happening in East London. I would point to the events of the weekend of 10 February 2001 as evidence that this is not the case.

In the weeks leading up to the Premiership matches of that weekend, the UK had experienced some of the wettest conditions in recent memory. Such is the standard of pitch maintenance at the top British grounds, players have become accustomed to performing on near perfect surfaces, whatever the vagaries of the climate. But even the most experienced ground staff couldn't prevent the constant downpours turning their genetically enhanced turf into a sea of mud. This was routine in the 1970s but presented a challenge to the newer breed of super-athletic footballers, whose game is more dependent on close ball control.

As I mentioned earlier, there appears to be a slight relationship between wet grounds and low goals. If this is the case the weather might provide a relating factor between different grounds.

One fact stood out for the eagle eyed - Premiership goals had slumped. Usually, top flight British football produces an average of 2.6 goals per game. But in the early weeks of 2001, goals had dried up - unlike the pitches. We were lucky to be getting 2.0 goals per game. Attackers were getting bogged down from the south coast to the North-East. Of course there was the possibility of other general factors coming into play - but it was the small chance that the ground conditions could play a role in every single game that was significant.

From a betting point of view, this presented intriguing possibilities. On the evidence of recent weeks it could be argued that the odds for an individual match containing fewer than three goals should have contracted. But clearly, on the basis of a small sample of recent games, this revision could only be minor.

Taking the 10 games that took place between Saturday and Monday of 10 February 2001, we would normally expect a rough 50-50 split between games containing more than two goals and those with less than three goals. In most series of 10 matches, the split would be 5-5, or 6-4, or more rarely 7-3. Very occasionally a split of 8-2 or 9-1, or the rarest, 10-0, would crop up. An accumulator on all 10 to contain fewer than three goals would pay about 1,667- 1.

But were the true chances of this result really so slim? I would argue that they were definitely not.

Semi-related bets do all sorts of strange things to the likely distribution of results. When there is a factor that could be producing an effect on a number of apparently separate events, there is an enhanced chance that there will be an extraordinarily odd result.

It is possible to spread bet on the number of goals in the English divisions and also to have a fixed-odds wager (with Stan James and others) on the total of Premiership goals. However, on this occasion, by far the most lethal form of attack was to line up odds on individual matches to finish with less than three goals into one enormous multiple bet so as capitalise on the possibility of a freak number of low scoring matches. Any eight from 10 selections requires 45 bets. Depending on the odds, nine correct returns around 3,402 units - all ten, a whooping 17,010 units.

On the weekend in question, nine out of the 10 matches resulted in fewer than three goals (only Everton v Leicester managed to produce more than two). This was an eventuality that, while not exactly a certainty, was well within the realms of possibility and a chance that was vastly more likely than the accumulative odds suggested.

Once a relating factor kicks in it has the ability to skew results in an extreme way. You could have legitimately argued that poor pitches would benefit attackers, causing a rush of goals. Paradoxically, an accumulative bet on all 10 matches to contain a high number of goals was, perhaps, also a good bet. We don't always need to know what effect a relating factor will produce. The fact that there is something in the background ready to pounce on all the matches should be enough to be alert to the possibility that an abnormal distribution of results is on the cards.

Any occasions where extreme weather will effect a number of grounds should make us think seriously about the possibility of having blanket multiple bets. In snow I would want to go against all the home sides; in hot, dry conditions I'd be looking to go high on goals in every match.

Aside from the weather, there is the issue of the relationships between different football markets. Here, Stan James are the company to watch like a hawk as they offer fixed-odds bets on the number of goals, corners, bookings, time of first goal, which side will take the first corner, and others. The degree to which any one of these markets is related to another is quite diabolically complicated. Some obvious combinations are not permitted to appear together in multiple bets, though I was somewhat surprised that you are allowed to combine a wager on the number of corners and the number of goals. At first sight I thought there may be a slight tendency for matches that contained low goals to also contain low corners. In the 28 Premiership 0-0 draws of 2000-2001, the average corners per match was 10.5. This was 0.4 below the overall mean for corners throughout the whole divisions, though the sample of matches is so small that the figure cannot be considered a particularly reliable estimate.

Both Stan James and William Hill offer bets on the attributes of live games. Both are quite happy to accept multiple bets on the number of bookings combined with the match score, but my figures suggest they shouldn't, as there is a very slight relationship between the number of goals in a game, and the disciplinary make-up - 0-0 draws tend to feature slightly fewer bookings (a mean make-up of 32.3) confirming that teams who settle for a bore-draw are slightly less likely to kick lumps out of each other.

Within a sporting context it is difficult to mathematically 'prove' the devastating power of a semi-related bet- with the above example it is difficult to quantify the exact effect of the bad pitches. However, if I use deliberately exaggerated example, where a numerical value can be imposed on the relating factor, it may help to convince you.

On the Thursday before a group of 10 Premiership matches, Joe Bloggs bookmakers chalk up prices on the number of goals in the Premiership games. Allowing themselves a reasonable margin, they go 10-11 for fewer than three goals and also 10-11 for more than two goals, in each of the 10 matches.

The FA then makes an extraordinary announcement. There is a possibility that for all the matches they will change the size of the goals - to dimensions of 4cms wide by 3cms high. (The ridiculous scenario allows us to introduce a quantifiable 'relating' factor into the 10 games.) Clearly, since the ball is larger than the goals there is not a hope of it entering the net, therefore it is an absolute certainty that no goals will be scored.

Joe Bloggs panic. They ask for clarification from the FA in order that they can frame odds. Under pressure the FA releases the fact that there is a 10 per cent chance that the mini-goals will be introduced. There is a sigh of relief from the Bloggs odds compilers, as they now seem to have enough information to produce odds. They calculate that, seeing as there is a 10 per cent chance of no goals being scored, there must be a 90 per cent chance of the games being 'normal'. Their new odds build in the 'mini-goal factor' using a simple weighted average of the possibilities.

They conclude, correctly, that there is now a 55 per cent chance that a single game will be low scoring and a 45 per cent chance that it will be high scoring. Building in a larger margin to protect themselves, they offer 4-6 for less than three goals and Evens for more than two goals. So long as punters bet only in singles Joe Bloggs is ensured to make a profit. However, there is one bet that could have the receivers knocking on the door - a 10-fold accumulator on every single match to finish in fewer than three goals.

It is easy to work out that in the event of the mini-goals being set up all round the country, there must be a 10 per cent chance that every single match will finish with no goals. Therefore the 'fair' price for this result can be no more than 9-1. Yet a 10-fold accumulator pays 165-1. The relating factor has caused the winnings to balloon to 18 times what they should have been.

This demonstrates the key principle to semi-independent bets. Just because the odds on a single event are 'correct' doesn't mean that the odds on the accumulative odds must also be in the bookies' favour.

If you take all the football odds on offer with one company it becomes evident that there must be a huge number of combinations of bets that should not be permitted, but this is rarely the case. I have consistently placed multiple bets, including on the internet, where there is a blatant relating factor. The principles are so blurred as to make it virtually impossible to come up with a set of rules that cover all eventualities.

A double on Liverpool to win the championship and their centre-forward to be top striker in the Premiership during the season is fairly obviously related. But how about their striker to be the season's top scorer in a double with Liverpool to beat Blackburn on Saturday?

When you start to mix in different sports, the inter-relationships of bets become amazingly entangled. Rain makes it more likely that a cricket Test match will end in a draw. It makes it more likely that horse racing winning distances will be large. It can negatively effect certain golfers from scoring a good round; and, believe it or not, there is even evidence that it causes the outside traps to win slightly more greyhound races (because the inside traps have to negotiate tighter turns and therefore have a tendency to skid around in the wet).

There is no way a cashier is going to start examining all these different possibilities to see if your multiple bet is technically allowable, and my reading of the larger firms rules suggests that they only have a hazy understanding of the area themselves. In all cases, any hint that there is a link between elements of a multiple bet is like throwing a bomb into the normally serene world of odds compilation. Usually we would be ecstatic if we to learn that, on any given bet, we were enjoying a few percent advantage over the odds. Semi-independent bets occasionally allow that advantage to be measured in terms of hundreds of percent over the bookmaker. As such they might represent the most lethal weapon in a punter's armoury.

chapter **sixteen**

# international competition strategies

The resurrection of football betting from the graveyard of ultra-high taxation in the late 1960s has needed little hype, though there is something slightly misleading about the much-repeated trumpeting of the turnover on the 1994 World Cup beating that of the Grand National. The romp around Aintree takes about 15 minutes, while the final stages of the FIFA World Cup are a twice-a-decade football overdose that occupies us for a full month.

The betting high-rollers come out in force for the event, with £50,000 plus bets on single matches becoming alarmingly commonplace. Most of those indulging in stakes of that magnitude are, I suspect, kindred spirits of the so-called 'whales' of Las Vegas - the type of person (invariably from the Far East) who wouldn't hesitate staking $20,000 on the spin of a roulette wheel for the sheer novelty of feeling reckless, having first insulated themselves in a cotton-wool mega-rich lifestyle.

On the face of it, the World Cup and the European Championship finals are probably not the best place to start a high-staking football betting habit. Just about every piece of information imaginable is available about the competing nations. The betting markets on the games themselves are so eagerly studied that any semblance of value rarely lasts five minutes. Not only is it the toughest stage for the teams, it is also a very stiff test of our gambling brains.

The World Cup, in particular, has developed on quite predictable lines. Prior to 2002 the format has managed to ensure that, even if the most entertaining nation in each competition doesn't win it, the most solid, technically proficient country is able to triumph. The lack of genuine upsets slightly surprises me. The

World Cup group stage, whereby two teams from four go through to the next round, is not exactly a league season. The three games that each team play should be barely enough for the 'best' team to assert its overall strength.

In fact, by the time it gets to the final round of group games, the situation is still almost chaotic - with just two matches played each, it is usually possible that any of the four teams in the group can finish in any of the placings within it. So you get the complex position of something like Argentina needing only a draw to qualify if Portugal win - but if Portugal lose by more than two goals, then Cameroon may qualify instead because of their better goal difference.

Having survived their groups, qualifiers need to win three matches in order to secure a place in the final, with all the tension and potential for an upset that the 90 minutes/extra-time/penalties format should bring. And yet genuine shocks on the World stage are few and far between. Only Denmark, in picking up the European Championship in 1992, were really dark horse winners in the modern era. In fact a look at the recent history of the World Cup reveals that favourites have a habit of just managing to squeak through, despite many of the eventual winners losing a game along the way.

The first punting advice from this is to make sure you don't look at the structure of the groups in a too 'fixed' way. The final positions are liable to be completely mixed up compared to the pecking order of the seeds. The first seeds fail to win their groups in major championships more often than they manage to top their groups. The only recent exception was in 1998, where the first seeds had a comparatively easy passage.

Euro 2000 played its part in the evolution of major international competitions, marking a substantial break from the usual pattern. The most noticeable fact about the finals held in Belgium and Holland was that the goal count was considerably up. Though not particularly stunning at face value, the 2.67 goals per game (excluding extra-time) was a vast improvement on the very low scoring we have endured in many previous competitions. The European Championships hit the low of 1.92 per game in 1984, and though it bounced back to 2.73 in 1988, trudged along at 2.26 in '92 and a drab 2.06 in '96. We have become used to the same low scoring in the World Cup finals as well.

The immediate consequence of lack of goals is a glut of draws (the fewer goals scored, the more chance of the teams ending 90 minutes on the same number). This led ex-Racing Post sports editor Derek McGovern to suggest the theory that you should always look to back the draw during the group games. To an extent, this is true and invariably has worked in the tournaments in which there are few goals overall. If you had backed every match in the final stages of the two competitions to end in a draw for the last 20 years, you would probably be marginally ahead. But it is a bit of a chicken-and-egg situation... which comes first, few goals or lots of draws?

The general lack of goals in the final stages of their showpiece competitions is known to irritate FIFA, and with varying amounts of determination they have tried at times to introduce rule changes that benefit attackers and encourage goal-scoring opportunities. Many innovations, such as the lighter ball, introduced in 2000, have been back door attempts to get the goals flowing. Such changes, when introduced in the national leagues, tend to have a short-term effect in producing goals (for instance, the introduction of the 'no back pass' law); but once players get used to it the goal tally sinks again.

My suspicion is that eventually FIFA will get their way and we will be treated to a tournament where there are over three goals per game. If this is the case, the balance of results will be changed. In Euro 2000, Coral took a hammering because, generally, the favourites in each match won, leaving the high-rollers (who apparently had been blindly backing them) with a wad of cash. Draws weren't in the picture - in the 24 games, a £10 stake on each (£240) to be a draw would have yielded a return of £140.

You can certainly forget the final stages of major championships as a good platform for backing shock results. Despite the occasional turn-ups, notably Cameroon memorably seeing off Argentina at odds of 12-1 in the opening game of the 1990 World Cup, stakes on outsiders would have been frittered away. This leaves the rather unpalatable conclusion that, as far as the individual matches go, it is difficult to see much beyond the odds-on teams. A greater number of goals will probably slightly aid the bigger nations as their natural supremacy has more chance to show itself.

The major championships have one unique football betting characteristic - that the odds for all the group stage matches are published in advance. You can therefore have a bet on a side in their third group game before they have played their first two. The bookies don't know what will happen - but unfortunately neither do we. The one possible advantage is that there is likely to be a slight relationship between the result of the first team's group game and their last, though working out the precise nature of the relationship becomes quite involved.

The Scottish national team is a case in point - famed for losing to inferior opposition in at least one of their first two matches, they have a noble history of beating, or at least very nearly beating, the first seeds in the last game. If, by some miracle, Scotland were to sail through two matches, how would they perform in their last game? You may suspect that they'd succumb to an awful tanking. Though an over-generalisation, this example illustrates the fact that one result can slightly increase or decrease the likelihood of another.

If a first seeded team was to lose its opening match, does it make it more likely, less likely or about the same that they will lose their last game as well? In the case of basically 'good' sides who are under a lot of pressure to perform from the folks back home, I'd say they were slightly more likely to win their last game, as a positive result is almost certain to be necessary to progress to the knockout stage. If this is the case, then a double on the first seed to lose or draw their opening match, paired with them to win their last match, might be placed at odds that are slightly in our favour.

The case with the lesser seeds isn't as clear cut - in fact it might work the other way around. A third seed losing to a second seed may already be out of the competition by the time their last game comes around. Since they may be up against a side who have to beat them to progress, it may be that losing their first game makes it somewhat more likely that they will lose their third as well.

Italy, notorious for their slow starts to international competitions, reflect the fortunes of first seeds in each group generally - that of the giants of world football only gradually lumbering into action. The pattern for the fourth seeds tends to go the other way. They appear able to acquit themselves reasonably well in their first two games, only to suffer significant reverses in their final group match. Their motivation is such that they are able to compete with the big boys in their first two matches.

But, assuming they face elimination, their resolve collapses in the final game - especially if it is against the first or second seeds. However, I don't think this necessarily applies to their final match if it is against the third seeds, as they may have had this country in their sights as the only side they had a realistic chance of beating anyway.

The way in which the group stages pan out is dependent on a mass of motivational factors. There are rewards for those willing to get immersed in the complexities of the group stages. Because of the vast number of companies offering odds on the finals of major competitions, the margins are wafer thin. In the group stages, the best prices available rarely add up to over 100 per cent, so if you're choosy with the odds it is comparatively easy to bet at a margin that is technically in your favour.

If you want a punt on the outright winners, it is probably better to stick to the fixed-odds rather than the spreads, as the way in which the spread firms price their indices (offering, for example, quotes based on a 200-150-100-75-50-25 index) tend to be biased against buyers of individual countries - all the quotes are mathematically slightly too high. This, of course, means that the indices are ideal territory for anyone looking to sell a team (back it to do worse than expected). If you think you can identify the winner, it is invariably best to back them on the fixed-odds.

chapter **seventeen**

# exploiting pricing errors

Despite their sometimes unfounded optimism, punters frequently have too much respect for the abilities of the odds compilers. With a greater number of companies in the market, the greater the number of comparatively inexperienced odds compilers the industry has had to throw to the betting mob. There is a general impression that, though there may be occasional problems with the prices with individual competitors, the general structure of the odds is always in the bookies' favour.

This is a long way from the truth. Everyday, quite fundamental errors are made. Just as unwary punters are susceptible to falling into a host of betting potholes, bookies are liable to get caught out by particular statistical quirks that go unnoticed. There is quite a set pattern as to which principles bookmakers frequently trip up on. A number of particular difficulties crop up time and time again with different firms.

The following is a run-down on many of the loopholes I have found it easy to take advantage of. Some are, to my knowledge, available at the time of writing - others have been closed. But it is the principles that lie behind these loopholes that are important to take note of. Just as there will always be punters who will throw good money after bad, there will probably always be bookies who make critical errors with related bets, mean-median confusion, and a number of other frequently occurring difficult areas.

Fixed-odds football betting in this country was just about killed off in the early-60s by an extraordinary series of pricing errors by Hills and Ladbrokes. Although we tend to think of football betting on a continuing upward popularly curve, it has never been as popular in Britain as it was in 1964. In an attempt to kill of their commercial competitors the two companies became embroiled in an odds war. Matches were not priced up individually but, rather, odds were offered for clients achieving a fixed number of correct selections - such as 25-1 for selecting six results correctly.

In an attempt to steal the thunder of the phenomenally popular pools companies, prices on draws were particularly pushed out - in one case to as long as 100-1 for predicting just three. Draws were slightly less frequent than they are now, but, given a full choice of games, offering more than 50-1 for finding three draws was asking for trouble. On a series of weeks where draws were frequent, both companies lost sums that brought them to their knees. This faltering start to the modern history of football betting should provide plenty of comfort for punters.

In terms of modern day pricing errors there are plenty to choose from, but my personal favourite was provided by the now defunct William Hill Index between 1998 and 2001. The market was on the time of the fastest Premiership goal. Generally on a Saturday there are eight Premiership matches (with one live on Sunday and another on Monday).

During 1999 and 2000, Hills usually offered a quote of 6-7 minutes on the time of the fastest goal being scored. Having had a quick look at this price, would you rather be a buyer or a seller? I'd guess that most would firmly want to be on the buy side. It is quite easy to imagine yourself watching the scores coming in and not hearing of a goal much before the 15th minute.

Because of the apparent psychology of the irresistibility to buy, I was immediately intrigued by the prospect of selling. It was in late 1998 that I had my first few trades on this market, selling for small amounts, though at that stage I had no particular inkling that there was a permanent advantage in selling. It was only after a handful of wins that I really began to examine the market in more detail.

The first line of enquiry was simply to imagine that, instead of eight separate matches, there was just one 'mega-game' taking place. This game was essentially a composite of the individual matches. Assuming an average of 2.5 goals per game in a Premiership match, eight of them should produce 20 goals.

Imagine just one game with 20 goals in it - at what point would we expect the first one? The usual way is to do this is to divide the number of minutes in a game by the number of goals expected - in this case, 90 divided by 20 equals 4.5 minutes.

This calculation, though seemingly innocent, is badly flawed. In just about every published discussion I've set eyes on, this error creeps in. If 20 events are divided into 90 minutes a simple division produces the wrong answer. The proof of this is imagine a game where the best estimate of an event occurring is just one. So if it were the case that we were expecting just one goal in a football match we'd perform the same calculation as before to see at what point we'd expect this goal to occur.

It is fairly clear that if we are expecting just one goal in 90 minutes then the best estimate of the time of its occurrence must be half way through, 45 minutes (ignoring the complication of stoppage-time for a moment). Perform the calculation and something strange happens - 90 minutes divided by the number of goals (1) is... 90. This is obviously not right. It can't be the case that the best estimate is the very last minute of the game.

The solution that brings us back to the clearly correct answer of 45 is to add one to the number of events. In this case the best estimate is 90 divided by one plus one (two). Similarly, if we are expecting 20 goals in 90 minutes then the best estimate is 90 divided by 20 plus one (21). This produces an answer of 4.28. On the basis of this rudimentary analysis we are still miles below the sell point of six minutes.

But the estimate of 4.28 only applies if goals are equally distributed throughout the game. This, we know, is not the case. Close to 55 per cent of goals are scored in the second-half (disproportionately towards the end of the game), with only 45 per cent in the first-half. Even those that appear in the first-half are not distributed evenly over the first 45 minutes.

The last 10 minutes of first-halves produce more goals than the first 10 minutes. It is relatively easy to build this in to the calculation. You simply need to imagine that the whole 90 minutes play takes on the goalscoring characteristics of just the first 10 minutes or so.

The first 10 minutes of matches produce about 22 per cent fewer goals than the 'average' minute. Therefore to get a truer picture we can knock 22 per cent of goals off our estimated tally of 20. This produces an adjusted total of 15.6. We can now say that the best estimate of the time of the first goal is 90 divided by 15.6 plus one (16.6), equals 5.42 minutes (or five minutes and 25 seconds).

So theoretically, the market was a definite seller. In practice it was even better. Because the average goals per games fluctuates markedly throughout the season it was possible to only trade when the seasonal averages were at their highest - i.e. at the beginning and end of the season. This meant that I eased off from late

November to early February but gave the market a hammering in other months. The result was it was possible to sell at six minutes for the eight games when the average goals per game were running at more like 2.7. The advantage here was over a whole point beneath the sell figure, netting substantial profits over a period of 18 months.

In February 2001, just weeks before their demise, Hills seemed to have worked out the market was permanently too high and finally adjusted their quotes down a point. But this market alone was my single biggest winner of recent times and was remarkably homework free - it was just a case of blindly selling week after week.

## accepting heavy downsides

I suspect that despite their pricing error Hills probably made a substantial profit out of the 'Fastest Premiership Goal' market for the simple reason that it would appear to take an awful lot of nerve to sell a market at six, with a maximum win of six points, where the possible loss was many times in excess of this. The worst I actually experienced was a make-up of 22 for eight games, though I managed to miss one nightmare make-up of 36 for a group of six European games.

I readily admit that the bet was, in practice, quite sickening. Listening to the radio for the first goal to appear was an exquisite form of torture, even though I knew for the sake of huge value that I had to put myself through it every Saturday.

The overall lesson from this sort of bet may be somewhat unpalatable to some, but I strongly recommend that you should always look to make the downside of a bet larger than the upside. In spread betting this means that the maximum potential winnings should be smaller than the maximum potential loss. On the fixed-odds you should try to avoid the open-ended side of any market - e.g. for fixed-odds bets on corners or goals, always look to go low. The reason for this is simply that just about everyone else is looking to bet on the open-ended side of a market. Prices are set accordingly, slightly in favour of those willing to risk higher downsides.

Spread firms experience their biggest losses in live matches that contain a high number of goals and bookings. Spread traders have gone on record as stating that their small staking customers (which sounds like a euphemism for long-term losers!) tend to win on games with loads of goals. The implication is that the serious professionals tend to go the other way and bet against the 'exciting' things happening, like a hat-full of goals or bookings.


## derived pricing errors

One interesting category of pricing errors is where a firm manages to twist a correct set of odds into an incorrect set of odds. Many markets on both the spreads and fixed-odds are derived from a fundamental quote or set of odds. A good example of this is the overall divisional goal supremacy bet offered by the spread firms - e.g. Division Two homes/aways 4.5-5.5 (the difference between the aggregate of the home teams' goals and the aggregate of the away teams' goals). The quote is effectively a combination of all the individual goal supremacy quotes on the games.

Occasionally something gets lost in the translation across to the derived market, which is where things can get very intriguing. Probably the longest standing loophole in football betting is contained within the handicap list on William Hill coupons. Most of the major firms present a list of 10-15 matches consisting mostly of seemingly very one-sided games where the home team is heavily odds-on. The away team is awarded a one-goal head start and the matches priced accordingly.

The three results (home win, draw, away win) on the handicap list now refer to completely different results in 'real life'. For the home team to win on the handicap list, it needs to win the game by two goals or more. A handicap list draw occurs when the home team wins by one goal. The handicap away win occurs when the home team fails to win the match (a draw or away win). It is in this last price bracket where the advantage to the backer lies.

The chance of the away team avoiding defeat must be derived from the company's assessment of their overall odds. For example, if the overall set of odds in the real game is 8-13 the home win, 12-5 the draw and 4-1 the away win, then the price for the away win on the handicap must very close to the total of the percentages for the 'real' draw and the 'real' away win. The associated percentages of the real draw (29.4 per cent) and the real away win (20 per cent) adds up to 49.4. This equates to just under Evens.

This has to be the correct price for the away win on the handicap list. But amazingly, Hills offer 5-4, a percentage of 44.4 per cent. This strange concession is offered to away backers on the handicap list presumably because it is primarily designed to attract shop punters into betting on dead-cert home teams to win by two goals or more. But the way in which it is priced offers a permanent advantage to those willing to oppose the obvious favourites.

Hills' handicap list particularly shines when the firm is offering the longest price on the away team to start with. Here the skewed pricing becomes even more magnified. If Hills offer the overall best price on the away team, over a range of companies (for example, so the best prices total 104 per cent), something intriguing happens when their handicap list price on the visitors comes into play. If you take the best price on offer on the home team and match it with Hills' handicap price on the away team, you have covered all three 'real' results.

But where Hills offer a handicap price, it is far enough out that the percentages of the two will always add up to less than 100 per cent. As only trebles and upwards are allowed with Hills' handicap list, this doesn't mean that it's practically possible to make an automatic profit by backing the two prices that make up all three of the match results - but it does give an impression of how screwy prices can be.

I recently surveyed the results of over 600 games that had featured on this list. Mathematically, it as clear that the margin in the backer's favour increased as the price on the away team got longer, and the results demonstrate this. Of 364 games where the away team on the list were offered at 11-8 and less (teams that are offered at 4-1 and less to win away on the standard long list), £10 on them all to have avoided defeat would have netted a return of £3,785.30, a performance of 103.98 per cent.

But where teams were priced at 9-2 and over on the long list, their handicap list prices of 6-4 and greater were proportionally more generous still. In this bracket there were 238 matches. A £10 stake on all of these would have returned £2,680, a performance of 112.6 per cent. This loophole is a close cousin of the 'fastest goal' opportunity in that the advantage is in doing precisely the opposite to what looks, on first inspection, to be the only realistic option. The actual bets on the handicap list where the backer's margin is greatest is where you can stomach backing very long odds away teams to frustrate the opposition - usually matches where the likes of Rangers and Arsenal are playing at home. Pricing errors almost never exist where they favour the types of bets that most punters are attracted to.

One of the pricing errors that I will always kick myself for not exploiting to a greater extent occurred with Ladbrokes prices for games to end in a draw after 45 minutes. In late 2000, I noticed that Ladbrokes invariably offered slightly longer odds than other companies on half-time draws to the extent that they were betting over-broke, especially on matches where one team was a strong favourite.

For quite a long time I dabbled with the usual trebles from eight or nine selections and got ahead fairly effortlessly. But what I managed to miss at the time was the fact that Ladbrokes prices were slightly incorrect all the way down the coupon - backing every single one to finish in a draw at half-time produced a profit most weeks. In this case I realised I shouldn't have been fiddling around with trebles at all, but opting for huge multiple bets in order to increase the advantage - any eight from 20, or even any 15 from 40 - though I suspect that a string of such winners may have alerted them to the fact that something was amiss with the odds.

## mean-median confusion

In the discussion on corners, I raised the issue of the important difference between the arithmetic mean and the mode in many betting markets. Aside from corners the principle also applies to the total number of goals in a game. We know that the average number of goals in British football is very close to 2.5. This might suggest that 50 per cent of games finish with three goals or more, and 50 per cent with two goals or fewer.

But as is the case with so many variables in football, there is a chance of scoring many above the mean, but the minimum number of goals scored in a game is only 2.5 below the mean (a 0-0 draw). The effect of this is that a slightly higher number of games finish with two goals or fewer than three goals or more. The fact that there are the occasional very high scoring games tugs the arithmetic mean upwards.

The figures reveal that the split is 54 per cent to 46 per cent in favour of two goals or fewer. As this breakdown isn't exactly difficult to find, you might expect that it would be plain sailing to produce baseline odds that reflect the true chances of games finishing within their price brackets. These could then be adjusted according to the circumstances of the particular game. In this case average odds of around 4-6 for two goals or fewer and Evens for three goals or more would seem to fit the bill.

But inspection of any coupon where these price brackets apply reveals that the odds are completely the wrong way around. Sitting in front of me, I have the

Tote's football coupon dated 9-10 March 2001, and in the low bracket only two out of the 10 games are at odds-on. The 'over' bracket is a string of skinny prices, ranging from 1-2 to a solitary Evens. These are so far out from the true frequencies that indiscriminately backing as many games as are up for offer to finish in two goals or fewer has to be the call.

But there have been ways to swing the margin even further in the backer's favour. The odds are adjusted around the wrong baseline figures - in the wrong way. It is assumed, broadly correctly, that games with very strong favourites will produce more goals than the average game, as it is more likely that a goal rampage is on the cards. But according to my analysis, the increased chances of a game resulting in more than three goals are overestimated in the odds.

The main culprits in this respect were Stanley Racing who, when they used these brackets, pushed the price out on two goals or fewer far too high in apparently one-sided games. The would frequently go as long as 13-8 for this bracket, despite plenty of evidence that the best teams do only marginally better in terms of getting involved in high scoring games.

Ladbrokes' current price brackets are sound, Hills like to offer 5-4 for two goals or fewer quite frequently, which makes them vulnerable. The Tote are on exceedingly dubious territory with their pricing, especially bearing in mind the possible relating factors, such as the weather, that might cause a sudden glut of low scoring games on the coupon. This leads me to believe that covering all the Tote's 10 games to end in fewer than three goals with trebles, and even small-stake eight-folds in addition, is a particularly lethal bet. A few of the smaller internet companies also offer this bet on individual games.

The mean-median confusion has interesting side-effects when we look at groups of games. If we consider just one game, then the chance of it finishing below the mean of 2.5 is somewhat greater than 50 per cent. But what are the chances of two games finishing below the expected mean of five goals, or for that matter the chances of 1,000 games finishing below the expected mean of 2,500 goals? This is worth considering as Stan James offer a bet on how many goals will be scored in particular divisions - e.g. for eight Premiership matches they might go 6-4 under 23, 7-4 for 23-27, and 13-8 for over 27. Hills also offered this bet for a while in 2001 but seemed to have given it up.

As we add more matches to the sample, the number of goals per game must regress to the mean. But the smaller the number of matches we look at the more chance that the overall mean will not be reached - remember that it is the occasional incidence of freak high scoring games that push the mean upwards. So long as these can be avoided in a small sample, then the mean tends not to be reached. The result is that whenever Stan James offer this bet on a group of divisional games such as the 12 that would normally occur on a Saturday afternoon, their prices on the under bracket are slightly more generous than they should be.

But the fun starts when there is just a small group of games, often on a Sunday. I have regularly got a price of 6-4 for a group of three games containing fewer than eight goals and occasionally even 13-8. If you base your calculations around the overall mean number of goals per game, there doesn't appear to be too much wrong here. If a spread company was to offer a quote of 2.4-2.7 on all three of the games, then the mid point is 2.55 - their true estimation. Multiplying 2.55 goals in each of three games gives an estimated total of 7.65. Here, there may not seem to be anything amiss with a price of 6-4 for fewer than eight goals.

I could tell you about the calculation for working out the correct estimation of goals in a given number of games, but it is hellishly complex to the extent that opening the spreadsheet on my computer (programmed by a particularly patient and Excel-literate friend) makes the processor threaten to pack up completely. The easier way of demonstrating that 6-4 is very generous price for three games to result in fewer than eight goals in simply to look at a series of football results and split them into groups of three.

It soon becomes evident that the 40 per cent implied in the odds of 6-4 is too low. For three games, the chance of them finishing with fewer than eight goals, based on a mean of 2.6 per game is 52.6 per cent, massively above the percentage implied in the odds. Again with this loophole, the value is in doing what the average punter would find unfulfilling - e.g. going low on goals. In fact by now it will probably have become quite clear that I'm a fully paid up member of the 'go low on everything' club.

## structural pricing problems

This catch-all category covers a multitude of pricing sins where there is a permanent opportunity to make a profit by betting in a certain fixed way. My deep interest in Australian football statistics was based around one key fact. The frequency of away wins in the Aussie State Leagues runs at 36-37 per cent, with home wins at 44-45 per cent and draws languishing on 18-19 per cent. But as far as the bookies were concerned, particularly Hills, away wins only happened about 33-34 per cent of the time. There was consistently a profit to be had in backing away teams. Clearly the home/away template that the firms were using for pricing these games was based too much on that of the British leagues, where the proportion of home wins is somewhat higher. But for the dedicated I still believe the Aussie odds are relatively easy to beat, even now that the away prices are somewhat less punter friendly.

I cannot believe that, of all the things we can bet on in the UK, there is a sporting endeavour that is more obscure and amateur in status than Australian Soccer. Even awarding it amateur status is quite generous as many of the players have to pay for the privilege of playing in the lower leagues.

In some of the matches that you may find yourself analysing the form book, the standard is on a par with pub football in the UK. Apparently it is quite common to find that the fixture list for a season has not been completed because some teams have simply 'forgotten' to play others. This is not to denigrate the Aussies - in fact it is somewhat astounding that, to my knowledge, there has never been the merest hint of match-rigging or other skulduggery.

Many teams have a very strong ethnic identity and, rather inevitably, tend to enjoy a good brawl with traditional national enemies. Some sides have strong links to the Yugoslav-Balkan area of Europe, so, knowing the intensity of bad feeling between different groups in the region, the ferocity of some of the Aussie rivalries is as intense as any local derbies in the world. This leads to very distorted patterns of results whereby utterly appalling teams (it is not unusual for double figure scores to be clocked up) manage to pull off a victory at huge odds against particularly loathed rivals.

The key to profiting on Aussie football is, first and foremost, never to bet on anything other than away wins. Secondly, try to keep to the lower divisions, particularly the Victoria leagues Division Four and Five, the Western Australian Second Division and the South Australian First Division. In these leagues the standard of football is at its lowest and the odds-compilers are still generous with the visitors.

Look for the merest hint of anything promising in an away side's current form. Even if they have a string of losses to their name, a semi-reasonable tally of goals is a promising sign. It is frequently possible to discover away sides at odds of more then 4-1 who are averaging well over a goal a game.

In my experience, these sorts of outfits are the most likely to land long odds. Odds-on away sides also provide good betting value - again, their goalscoring potential seems to be a key factor in picking out the bankers. Avoid strong away favourites if they have failed to score in any of their last four matches.

When I first looked at the summer Australian odds, it was a very rare chance to bet on a foreign league. These days it is commonplace for British bookmakers to price a huge variety of continental games. Hills offer odds on the Swedish, Norwegian, Israeli and Japanese leagues, to name just a few. Though I haven't examined these in detail, I would imagine that the potential is vast for structural pricing errors (where the home/away balance implied in the odds is incorrect). There has never been a better time to develop some expertise in foreign football.

## place-betting loopholes

Thankfully, the debate over whether each-way betting is inherently good or bad is mostly confined to racing. But there are a variety of football betting markets where it helps to know the ins and outs of the mysteries of the each-way bet, from pre-season divisional betting to relegation markets at the very end of the season. Each way betting, where you have to have a stake on the win part that is at least equal to that on the place part, is an inflexible way of offering odds on a competitor gaining a place.

The way in which place odds are imposed, by dividing the odds on the win part by a fixed fraction, generally one-fifth or one-quarter, usually works against the backer. But the rigid way in which the formula is imposed does not take into account the win odds relative to each other - a critical part of formulating the true chances of an individual competitor gaining a place. This can lead to a number of intriguing betting possibilities.

The key to understanding each-way betting is to look at the two parts of the bet independently. You can get tied in knots by trying to mix up the two to determine the possible profit potential of a bet. The win part is easy to assess. Imagine you fancy backing Wrexham at 20-1 each-way to win their division. It is straightforward to assess the over-round built into the prices on the win part. The total of all the percentages of the teams in the division might add to 130 per cent. To see whether there is any value in the place part of the bet you need to look at the over-round that applies to the place odds.

If the bookie is offering one-quarter of the odds for the first three teams, then we can say that, with three places, fair place odds would add up to 300 per cent. Similarly, if they were paying four places, then fair odds would add up to 400 per cent. Adding the percentages associated with the place odds allows us to discover the over-round. In Wrexham's case one-quarter of 20-1 is 5-1 (16.7 per cent).

It is remarkable how much variation there is in the over-rounds on place odds. Often the margin built into the place odds will be greater than that in the win odds. A win bet in a market with an over-round of 113 per cent may be bearable, but by betting each-way on the same market you could potentially be exposing yourself to an over-round on the place odds of more than 130. Unless you are absolutely convinced there is something ridiculously wrong with an individual price, this makes it a very dubious prospect.

Where the favourite is offered at odds-on there is frequently the opportunity to benefit from generous each-way prices. As an extreme example, imagine if there was a league that contained Arsenal and nine pub sides. Since it is virtually certain that Arsenal would win, we can assume their odds would be around 1-50. The pub teams are all offered at 80-1. This adds up to an overall percentage of about 110 on the win part.

But without having to churn through the sums, it is fairly clear there is a massive advantage in favour of the backer on the place part of any bet on this fantasy division. If the place odds were one-fifth the win price for the first three places, then it is 16-1 that any one of the pub teams will achieve a place. Two of them must place, even when Arsenal win. Ten pounds on all of them at the place odds risks a total stake of £90. Two of them will place at 16-1, so the total return must be £340. There is a 10 per cent margin in favour of the bookie on the win part of the bet and at least a 350 per cent margin in favour of the backer on the place part.

Although we cannot expect anything quite this spectacular to occur in real life, there is at least one recent example of this place betting loophole. With Manchester United dominating the Premiership, pre-season odds in 2001-2002 featured them at various shades of odds-on. The fixed-odds division of Sporting Index, Sporting Odds, priced Manchester United at 8-11, offering one-quarter of the odds for the first four. This resulted in a margin in the backer's favour of 25 per cent on the overall place odds. Of course, with each-way betting you have to halve your stake at the win odds, so 50 per cent of your stake is tied up where there is a significant over-round. However, if you want a bet that is conceivably in your favour overall, it is well worth keeping a hawkish eye on the structure of place odds.


# spotting related bets

The introduction of spread betting threw down many challenges to the traditional fixed-odds industry. The new breed of spread punters developed a sudden fascination for the number of goals, corners and bookings that appear in the game - an area that had never been explored by the fixed-odds firms. Having realised that they could muscle in on the act, fixed-odds firms started to offer odds on these subsidiary markets. If the spread firm could offer a quote of 11-12 for the number of corners in a game, the fixed-odds firms simply build their odds around the market.

This appears straightforward enough, though, as we have seen, the fixed-odds companies faced the challenge of needing to base their prices around the median of values rather than the spread companies concentrating on the arithmetic mean. They didn't make the transition very well, a laxness that still can be punished today, but there was a further and potentially even nastier smelling difficulty around the corner.

In spread betting there is no such thing as a multiple bet. For them and us, this simplifies matters considerably. But the fixed-odds firms have always seen them as a route to higher profits. But when you try to mix the concepts of multiple bets with fixed-odds on football's subsidiary markets an almighty mess ensues. In 1999, Ladbrokes, the traditional 'safe pair of hands' in the UK betting industry, stepped in it up to their necks.

When I first set eyes on Ladbrokes' Matchstats section of their football coupon in late 1999, it was a moment of revelation. I had long suspected that some pricing 'errors' weren't necessarily errors at all. If a company wanted to offer over-generous prices on a game finishing with fewer than three goals, perhaps they knew what they were doing.

Since all the money taken by them was probably on the high side by those who wanted to put their feet up and cheer on goals in a live TV game, I wondered whether the prices were too generous on the low side because they simply wanted to try to balance the books - i.e. masses of the not-so-clued-up go high for small stakes and a few go low for large stakes.

But 'Matchstats' must have been an unintended howler. The bet itself allowed the backer the chance of a four-fold on some of an individual game's characteristics - the number of goals, the number of bookings (using the spread companies' 25-10 scoring mechanism), the number of corners and the match result. For each leg of the bet there were three choices. For goals, perhaps 12-5 for two, 9-4 for exactly two and 10-11 for over two.

Likewise, bookings and corners were also split into three price brackets, with the home win, draw and away win at the bottom, to complete a neat looking 3 x 4 table of different prices. It is the existence of the first and the fourth legs that initially amazed me. They were inviting you to have a bet on the result of the match combined with the number of goals it would contain. This leads to one observation immediately - some combinations are wiser than others. How can you have a draw in a game with over two goals? Not very easily is the obvious answer, as you only have the rare 2-2 or 3-3 in your favour.

However, a game that contains exactly two goals is quite likely to end in a draw at 1-1. In this case, multiplying the two sets of odds for 'exactly two goals' and 'draw' was inevitably always much higher than you'd receive for a 1-1 correct score bet. By backing the away team at 5-1 to win and the game to finish in fewer than two goals, you were effectively hoping for a 0-1 scoreline. This was a 10-1 chance on a correct score bet - but it ballooned to more like 20-1 when the odds of the two legs of the Matchstats bet were multiplied together. This particular combination came into its own when Scotland beat England 1-0 at Wembley in a European Championship qualifier, a game for which a Matchstats coupon was published.

The result of the match and the number of goals it contains are clearly related. It was just a question of sticking to the combinations of bets where the mulitplied odds were more than the true chance of that combination. Then it was just a question of sitting back and waiting for that particular combination to appear, to receive a vastly inflated payout.

At first, I got excited about the fact that there was probably a relationship between the number of goals and the number of corners in a match. It seemed to make sense to back low goals in combination with low corners, though I now know that the two are only very faintly related. In fact this didn't really matter, because with the bookings and corners leg of Matchstats, Ladbrokes had fallen into the other trap of offering fixed-odds prices on subsidiary markets - mean-median confusion.

The result was that, rather majestically, the other two legs of the bet were easy to call. Under 12 corners was sometimes as high as 11-8, an extraordinarily generous price for something that happens much less than 50 per cent of the time. The price for the low bookings bracket was similarly set far too high.

In its lifetime of around nine months, the Matchstats bet yielded me an 80 per cent profit on stakes, without ever considering the relative merits of the teams involved. I doubt that anything like it will ever appear again, but there is still huge scope for legitimately placing related bets.

chapter **eighteen**

# the rough guide to staking

Taking everything that has ever been written about gambling, the subject of staking and staking systems has been done to death. This is possibly a throwback to casino gaming where, as all the games that are played against the house are basically a matter of pure chance, the subject of staking was really the only subject there was to discuss. And even then, most of it was relatively useless. No staking strategy can turn a bad gambler into a good one. It is possible, however, that a good staking strategy can turn a good football gambler into an even better one.

The first point to bear in mind about staking is that whether or not a particular type of bet or stake level is right for the individual punter all comes down to his overall performance level. Take two imaginary punters. The first is a mug of such magnitude that he hardly ever finds a single winner. Such is his almost supernatural ability to put money on the wrong teams, he only retains 30 per cent of all his stake money. What should his staking strategy be?

Clearly he should stake the absolute minimum possible on every bet, preferably nothing at all, as the more he gambles the more he loses. Perhaps we can say that he should bet the minimum stake possible to sustain an interest. Technically he shouldn't touch any multiple bets whatsoever because the bigger profit margin that is built in to them will ensure that he loses quicker.

At the other end of the performance scale, Mr Shrewdie has the ability to pick winners in his sleep. As such he maintains an incredible 200 per cent performance level. Assuming for a moment he is allowed to get his stakes on at a bookie, he shouldn't bother having any money in a building society, nor should he have to endure the drudgery of work. His punting talents are such that, in order to get very rich very quickly, he should gamble as much as possible. There is no point in him having too much cash hanging around, as it would be better spent on betting. There is only one proviso with this - even though he has a magnificent record, he is liable to face a significant losing run at some point.

This he has to build into his staking plan. If he puts every last penny he has on Bury on a wet Wednesday night, and they lose, he is bust. So in order to maximise his winnings he needs a reasonable sized fighting fund to sustain relatively lean spells. He can use whatever multiple bets he wants, from Lucky 15's to Round Robins. His basic ability is so good that he should probably place multiple bets very liberally, as they will significantly boost his winnings.

The only warning here is that he shouldn't get too carried away with how many selections he puts in single line of a multiple bet. It is theoretically possible for him to lose permanently in some extreme circumstances. If he changed his staking so that all ever did was to compile lines of 15 selections in an accumulator he may never actually win anything, even though he maintained a fantastic ability to pick the right ones.

In an annoyingly simplistic way, these are the only staking facts that really matter. It is very difficult to judge how anyone should stake their bets without knowing how good they are at finding winners. But for the purpose of this discussion, I'll assume we are talking about someone who has a performance level of around 100 per cent. With some categories of their bets they are above the magical 100 per cent performance level, with others they are below it. This is the pattern for a considerable number of reasonably good football bettors.

The most obvious thing to do in these circumstances is to get rid of the types of bets that are dragging down the performance level. I know it may seem to some like a drab mantra, but I'm afraid the "keep a written record of your bets" phrase has to be wheeled out. It can be a pain, but it is remarkable how inspection of actual betting records reveals strange truths about betting performance that you may never have guessed at.

In general I have always been surprised at the fact that my system bets tend to be more successful than those where I have consciously tried to pick the winner. 'System' bets are where I had no particular view about the contest itself but felt the odds on one of the outcomes were over-generous. Bets where I was simply predicting a particular result produced a far worse performance.

The pattern will vary from person to person, but keeping a written record of bets allows you ruthlessly to ditch any tactics that are not paying off and concentrate on more successful areas. There is always pressure, from amongst things books like this, to feel that it is vital to be develop a detailed knowledge of all areas of betting. But if you're good at one area, don't waste your time mucking around with others. The bookings market, for instance, has next to nothing to do with other football markets. If you don't want to get involved with disciplinary markets then you shouldn't dip in to them occasionally. Simply ignore them altogether.

Most gamblers try their hand at a variety of sports - there's nothing inherently wrong with this but make sure you are not trying to spread the net too wide. If you're genuinely a dab hand at Formula One betting, then by all means keep plugging away, but otherwise steer clear of any territory where you are merely dabbling because it happens to be on TV.

# proportional staking

There is a legitimate debate about whether we should stake 'proportionally' (so that all bets have a similar potential win figure) or whether it is better to stick to the same sort of stake level regardless of its price. Imagine you sit down on Saturday morning and identify two different bets. The first is Coventry to win a cup-tie at home at a price of Evens, the other is a 100-1 shot on Wigan to win the competition - though the reasoning behind this bet needn't bother us for now.

If you put £20 on each, the significance of the Wigan bet becomes hugely magnified as you are looking at a potential win figure of £2,000 - 100 times the amount that you could win on Coventry. The Coventry bet is completely dwarfed in terms of its relative importance.

Broadly you should aim to vary the stake on single bets according to the potential win figure. So if your return target figure is £200 then the stake on an Evens chance should be about £100; a 1-2 shot, £150; and a 20-1 bet, more like £10. This ensures that all bets become equal in importance. On the point of staking, a lot of betting writing becomes unnecessarily detailed. We are told to stake exactly £36.56 on a selection because it is mathematically correct in the circumstances. This is frequently technically true, but the only time you really need to worry precisely about the stake figure is if you are trying to hedge another bet, or attempting fixed-odds or spread betting arbitrage.

On a similar theme, I don't get too strung up about the concept of a betting bank, the size of which is supposed to determine the stake on the next selection.

Worrying too much about the preciseness of staking eats up valuable time that could be spent more productively.

For those interested in such areas, the 'Kelly Strategy' provides a definitive guide to mathematically correct staking. It highlights the key principle that you should stake according to the size of your advantage - this harks back to my first example about the two gamblers at either end of the performance spectrum.

Clearly, all bets are not the same in terms of how confident you are in their potential. We all know that there are a handful of occasions where we would like to sell all our possessions and get a bank loan in order to raise the stake for some particularly stand-out bet, whereas at other times we are well aware that a certain wager is just a vague stab in the dark.

Discussion of betting matters inevitably uses some phrases that hint at numerical values, but not too explicitly. What, for example, is an 'excellent chance' of Leeds winning? It sounds a bit like 70 per cent or so. How about a 'moderate prospect' - 40 per cent? Using broad, subjective phrases to describe the chance of something happening can lead to trouble, particularly when assessing the likelihood of things turning against us, such as the chance of a huge spread betting loss.

Everyone tends to be over-optimistic when guessing at the result of a bet. If you have sold the bookings market it is quite easy to make wildly inaccurate estimates of the true chance of a large make-up. You may grudgingly admit to the prospect of five bookings, but remain stubbornly resistant to the possibility that one, two or more players could be sent off.

A useful word in betting is 'conceivable'. We can say that the conceivable scenario contains 95 per cent of the possible results - or, in spread betting terms, make-ups. On this basis we will have to ignore the possibility of a mega-freak make-up on the high side. If we stake with the idea in mind that the make-up could be 240, we'd be too nervous ever to bet at all.

However, the figure of 100 probably does fall within the range of 95 per cent of make-ups - it's not so extraordinary that you shouldn't consider the possibility. You needn't start drawing graphs to get to this figure - a good guess is sufficient. Theoretically a losing run of bets could be infinite, but we can imagine a conceivable losing run (one which ignores the most extreme five per cent of cases) is about five when betting at odds of around Evens.

To achieve some semblance of ordered staking, I assign every bet to one of three categories depending on how optimistic I am. An average fixed-odds bet would look for a return of around £250; a mini-bet around £100; and, rarely, a maxi-bet in the region of £600. The actual figures are of no importance - to some they may look quite large, to others, pitifully small. It is the fact that there is some degree of thought about the bet's status that is the important point. The process of deciding which category any given bet fits into is useful in quantifying how I really feel about it.

## multiple bets

The level of staking on a single bet is relatively easy to apply, but much of football betting has to revolve around the thorny subject of multiple bets. The level of stake on a multiple bet is tricky enough, but knowing which multiple bet to have in the first place is more difficult still. It is possible that, within a short time, unrestricted singles will be permitted on all matches. But even then we will be left with a 'trebles and upwards only' rule on speciality bets that we feel we may have an advantage over. So, for the foreseeable future, we will probably still need a grounding in the subject.

The area of multiple bets is often treated as being somewhat more exciting than it really is. You will have probably read all sorts of things about how one multiple bet is better than another. For instance: "This bet combines a banker selection with two at longer odds guaranteeing a return if you can correctly predict just one out of three scorelines."

The claims made for certain types of bets are true in a sense, but in essence all multiple bets are as good or bad as each other. Whatever strange concoction of doubles, trebles and bankers you put in a bet, the potential of each new configuration simply changes according to the overall performance level.

Let's say you have picked out six selections all at 3-1. Two of them are correct, so assessing your performance in terms of singles, you would have staked six units for a return of eight units. At this level of performance multiple bet 'A' might return you very little, whereas multiple bet 'B' might return you a substantial sum. But had you managed to find three winners instead of two, then 'B' would have paid much more than 'A'.

Occasionally I hear circular arguments develop between customers in betting shops on this point. One will say, "My Yankee will pay much more than your Lucky 15, because if I get three selections correct I'll win £43. But you'll only get £32 for exactly the same winners." This debate can go on for ages because each multiple bet rewards different types of performance level. But, with one or two odd exceptions, all multiple bets are basically the same. Since we are required to bet mostly in trebles, it is this combination that we need to concentrate on. To illustrate a key principle to using multiple bets successfully, let's say you have identified six selections, all at 2-1, that you want to bet on. How about throwing caution to the wind and having a six-fold on the whole lot? It's easy to say that this is a bit dim because the chances of it happening are so remote, but then again the chances of it happening are reflected in the payout you will achieve, so in some ways this is not actually a fair argument.

The short-term objection to this bet is that you are going to have to wait too long to get any sort of reward for your efforts. If you get four of the selections correct, you have achieved a performance level of 150 per cent (six units staked with nine returned). But you haven't received a penny back for your endeavour. If you keep betting at this level of performance you will, one day, get all six correct, and you be waiting far less time than someone with a worse performance level. But in the meantime you might have gone broke in trying.

You should therefore try to ensure that you get some sort of return if you achieve a good performance level (a profit if the bet was assessed as placing six singles). To achieve a return you must find three winners out of six (a 150 per cent performance level). There are 20 trebles in six selections. If you get three correct you will receive a return of 27 units (one treble correct at odds of 2-1, 2-1 and 2-1 again). Here you receive 135 per cent of your initial stake back, not as good as the 150 per cent you would have got had you placed singles, but at least it keeps your head above water.

With four correct, the multiple bet shoots ahead in terms of its rewards. If you'd placed singles, your six-unit stake would return 12 units (a performance of 200 per cent). But here the trebles come into their own. Your 20-unit stake would yield four correct trebles, each paying 27 units - in total a monster payout of 108 units, or a return of 540 per cent of your stake. This amply illustrates the point that multiple bets reward a good basic performance much better than singles, but they also unduly punish us for a poor or even slightly above average performance. It is this last facet of them that we need to try to minimise.

The key point is that a multiple bet should give us a return if we would have made a profit by backing the selection in singles. If it doesn't, we can get stuck in the rut of being able fundamentally to beat the bookie but fail to get a return regularly. It multiple bets are badly thought out, it is actually possible to lose money permanently; whereas, had the same bet been placed in singles, the punter would have been ahead.

This principle instantly rules out a vast number of types of multiple selections. Quite frequently, on the back of coupons, you will see a multiple bet suggested that relies on 'full cover'. For instance, it might suggest backing six selections in trebles, four-folds, five-folds and an accumulator, all to the same stake.

This type of bet should always be swerved, as it is clear your return for a basically reasonable performance will be hopelessly tiny. In this case, if you got three selections correct (a 150 per cent return on stake if the bet were singles) the 42-unit stake you would need for a full cover bet would only return nine units, a paltry nine per cent of stakes. The rewards for getting the whole lot right are astronomical, but you may be sleeping on the street before you hit the big one.

Aside from straight full cover bets, this rules out all the variants that tend to be heavily promoted in betting shops, from Goliaths, Lucky 31s to Yankees. This leaves us with the option of trebles from a given number of selections.

| Number of selections | 4 | 5 | 6 | 7 | 8 | 9 | 10 |
|---|---|---|---|---|---|---|---|
| Number of trebles required | 4 | 10 | 20 | 35 | 56 | 84 | 120 |

In the vast majority of cases this is the only configuration of multiple bets that you need to bother about. The vast majority of the multiple bets I place are either 'trebles from seven selections' or 'trebles from eight selections'. Unless the matches are particularly long-odds away teams these bets ensure that the principle of getting a return for a reasonable overall performance is maintained.

Despite what many would still like to have us believe, particularly those who advertise miracle betting systems in the press, there is absolutely no way that by varying stakes you can put yourself ahead long-term. If your performance, when assessed as singles, is under 100 per cent, it is impossible to vary stakes in order to achieve a long-term profit.

## draws are a drag

Draws can be annoying things at the best of times, but if you bet often enough you are bound to come across possibly the most unpleasant of all football betting experiences - the unwanted draw accumulator. This is most likely to happen when you have identified a number of away sides at apparently attractive odds. You back them only to find that the whole lot result in draws. Despite the fact you were correct in identifying that your chosen sides could frustrate their opponents, you have failed to win a penny. To try to illustrate what is happening here, imagine a game between West Ham and Sunderland, where the odds are 4-5 West Ham, 11-5 the draw, 3-1 Sunderland. Visualise the chances of West Ham winning as if they were plotted on a straight line

---

**100 per cent West Ham win      Draw      100 per cent Sunderland win**

Before the match, if we had to mark a point along the line that was our estimate of where the result would fall, we would, according to the odds, place it just to the left of the draw portion in the middle. If West Ham perform slightly better than expected, they must win - the estimate of the result is dragged slightly to the left, further into their winning territory. But if they perform slightly worse than expected, the estimated result is dragged into the middle draw portion.

This may seem an overcomplicated way of explaining the patently obvious (that poor home teams are forced into draws) but it does illustrate the fact that whenever you back an away team your selections have to be good enough to avoid the cavernous draw portion in the middle. Quite naturally you can find yourself lumbered with a whole load of them.

Newer forms of handicap betting give the opportunity to avoid this syndrome. The best is probably Hills' system of awarding one of the teams a half-goal, or one-and-a-half-goal head start. (This is different to the handicap list on their standard coupons and is currently available on their website; though, at the time of writing, not in their shops.) By artificially awarding handicaps in units of half a goal, there can never be a draw result. If you want to back a longer-priced away team to do well, you simply have to back them with a handicap - you get a return if they win or draw.

Otherwise, we are somewhat stuck with dreaded draws. As far as I know, there is virtually no way of actually predicting them, but equally they are very difficult to avoid. I have tried a variety of methods of backing draws with positive results, but none particularly thrill me. You could place a bet that combines, for instance, draws and away wins in the form of "any three from seven to result in a draw or away win". To cover three selections for both results requires eight lines, multiplied by "any three from seven" (35 lines) giving a grand total of 280 lines. But it all gets very messy.

# blind alleys

Most readers will know of the infamous system of doubling up after a loser, and its variants - many paradoxically recommend increasing stakes after a winner. Some recommend betting to a target win figure and going back to an initial stake. They are all a total waste of mental effort, though why they are a waste of mental effort is the most interesting thing about them.

The 'doubling up' system is a subtle con because its plays on our inability to perceive the possibility of a very long losing run or a freaky sequence of results. By doubling up stakes it looks like you are making small gains consistently with no risk. In fact you are making small gains at the considerable risk of hitting a long losing run, beyond which you cannot possibly stake as you will have run out of funds.

Losing, and indeed winning, runs strike a lot more frequently and with more ferocity than we tend to imagine. In preparing this book I witnessed a strange example of this (though thankfully it didn't cost me anything). I was examining whether there was any mileage in a theory that has been doing the rounds for a few years. Recounted by Derek McGovern in the *Daily Mirror*, the theory states that when Ladbrokes are offering the best price for a particular team, you should back their opponents. Supposedly, this is because Ladbrokes employ the best odds compilers, so when they go long on a certain team, you can probably assume there is value by taking the best price with another firm on the other team.

To look at this I took a season's results and looked at the consequences of backing any team where Ladbrokes were, on their own, best-priced on their opponents. Using the Racing Post Pricewise column (that compares the prices of five of the leading British bookmakers), I jumbled up the season's sample of results to try to randomise the order in which I examined each week.

By the time I had noted down the result of the 100th game where Ladbrokes were best-priced, a staggering pattern had set in. Just as the theory suggested, when Ladbrokes were longest for the home team, the away team appeared to out-perform their odds. A string of 4-1s. 9-2s and more were appearing, to such an extent that a pound on all the target sides was performing to 126 per cent of stakes.

The pattern didn't let up as the sample increased to 160 games. This, I began to suspect, was an absolute pearl of a football betting system. But after the 160th result, the whole pattern changed. Suddenly it seemed, not a single team that was opposed by Ladbrokes managed to win. This new pattern set in with a vengeance and was still dominant by the 300th result. On the basis of this evidence I would have to say that the 'back those that Ladbrokes oppose' theory doesn't work - though for a long period of rooting through a random sample of games, it did.

The lesson here is that, even in seemingly quite large samples of matches, series of results creep in that are not statistically representative of all games. There are formal mathematical rules about error in sampling, but as a rule of thumb guide I have found that anything under a sample of 300 games tends to be unreliable. Bearing this principle in mind, it is not worth getting too hung up about the significance of you own winning/losing runs on the basis of a small number of results. The fact that we tend to underestimate the extent to which odd-looking sequences appear means that we are unduly pessimistic about a nasty run of losers but also too joyous about a few winners. Don't be too hasty to change general strategy or staking on the basis of a past few results.

chapter **nineteen**

# the £100 challenge

So does everything in the preceding chapters actually work? This is an account of how my gambling went on one particular Saturday - an attempt to win a reasonably modest target of £100 from football betting. Writing at this moment, I have no idea how it will turn out. It is not a retrospective account. The contents of this chapter have been inserted in bite-size pieces over three days. I will include it, win or lose.

Saturday 12 January 2002 happens to be the last weekend before the book is due at the publishers. I was aided by a close betting companion, who stayed over to take part in the punting deliberations. The target of winning £100 was not entirely arbitrary. I would normally risk around £1,000 for a day's betting, including conceivable spread betting losses - so a 10 per cent profit target was simply derived from this staking figure.

Although I am presenting this as a typical Saturday, there did appear to be a standout opportunity with a handful of games, so my expectation was that the results might fall better than usual. Then again, most of us tend to fantasise that every Saturday is going to be the one that provides the massive windfall.

Although I only have scant evidence for a link between the weather and football results, I tend to categorise a forthcoming Saturday as having potential for a low or high number of goals depending on the weather forecast. The previous Saturday had seen many postponements of FA Cup third round ties due to frost. But within the space of four days, it had become far milder. If there is anything in my theory that a quite sudden change of conditions causes the goal count to fluctuate, then the forthcoming weekend should be quite good for goals. Before I'd looked at any of the individual games, I'd already considered having a few spread bets on the basis of the number of goals in each division being comparatively high.

Aside from this rather woolly strategy, by Thursday I have a strong feeling about two other principles that I plan to exploit. The first concerns the hangover effect that might afflict teams who managed a surprising win in the FA Cup last week. There are four matches that fit into the 'giant-killers' bracket. In a particularly bad-tempered affair, Cardiff City beat Leeds with a last minute goal on Sunday, and face Peterborough at home this Saturday. Bristol Rovers went to Premiership Derby and came away with a 3-1 win. First Division West Brom beat Sunderland. And Leyton Orient, having won at Portsmouth on Saturday, face the trek to Carlisle.

I'd looked at the results of games that FA Cup giant-killers had played immediately after their success during competitions in the previous three seasons. Their record was particularly poor. Of 14 sides who'd won in the cup the previous game, only two had gone on to win their next match; and it was noticeable that these rare winning sides had a considerable break between the cup-tie and their next league game.

I had already been scuppered by a rather large oversight. Somehow I managed to miss the fact that Bristol Rovers had been scheduled to play a derby match with Bristol City on Wednesday, just four days after their FA Cup triumph. I have only got to realise this from today's (Thursday) paper. Rovers lost 0-3 without me ever realising. This leaves three 'post giant-killing' matches left for Saturday.

The other theory I have about Saturday's round of games is that there might be an unusual pattern of results in the Premiership. For some reason, the matches taking place this weekend are the reverse of fixtures played just three weeks ago. So, for example, Everton entertain Sunderland, even though it is only 21 days since they lost 0-1 at Roker Park. I have a quick attempt at looking up the results of the games where there was a similar pattern to the fixtures in previous seasons, but give up quickly, having not been able to find a precedent for this.

My line of thinking is based solely on an interview I'd seen with a Sunderland player, who suggested that sides tended to be more motivated when they played teams they had previously lost against earlier in the season.

It was as though having someone do the double over you was especially humiliating and to be avoided at all costs I reasoned that if this was true, where the reverse fixture was played relatively quickly, this effect might be greater than normal. I considered the possibility of betting on teams who had lost the previous reverse fixture. Of course, this was more or less the opposite of what other backers might do. The form lines are relatively fresh.

Having had the same games played just three weeks ago between roughly the same sets of players, it would be easy to deduce that, whatever the previous result, we might expect more of the same this weekend. But the motivation-to-avenge-a-recent- defeat theory went in the opposite direction.

❏ ❏ ❏

Friday's *Racing Post* gives the first listing of odds on offer for Saturday. Examining the Premiership, I begin to have second thoughts over one of the selections. Blackburn had unexpectedly won at Charlton in their league match three weeks ago. According to my thinking, Charlton might be at over-generous odds to turn the tables at Ewood Park.

But the best price on offer was just 2-1, considerably more skinny than I'd hoped. Charlton have propelled themselves up to a very respectable eighth place in the table - but mostly off the back of some exceptional wins against other London teams, where their motivation as the poorer London cousins of the likes of Chelsea and Arsenal had got them particularly fired up. I'm not sure this applies outside London, so am tempted to swerve them on Saturday.

I decide that Tottenham, who went down in their reverse fixture at Ipswich three weeks ago, don't look very suitable to back as they've had a tough Worthington Cup semi-final against Chelsea in midweek.

This leaves Aston Villa, Bolton, Everton and Leeds (the first three at home) as qualifiers for my avenging-a-recent-defeat theory. At this stage I'm not sure how to back them. Bolton, who lost to Chelsea in the reverse fixture, also fit the theory. But motivation or not, I have no stomach to support them at home. With a small number of games the spread companies mini-performance indices are always tempting, though I confess to having quite a poor record on them compared to the fixed-odds.

❏ ❏ ❏

The four Premiership contenders and the FA Cup hangover teams bring the total of backable sides to seven - quite enough for one day. By Saturday morning, I am ready to think more about the 'high goals' bet. The day has brought glorious weather - or at least as glorious as any day in mid-January can muster. At first I consider buying the divisional goals spreads to a small stake - possibly £10 per goal for each division.

On examining the spread companies' pages we discover IG's 'Fastest Premiership Goal' spread is pitched at 7-8 for the eight games kicking off at 3.00pm. There is a rather tortured history to the offering of this market. When William Hill Index folded, it was still offering the bet at what I was sure was too high a price. When IG took over their customer base, they continued offering the market, though for much of the time it was priced, if not correctly, less incorrectly than Hills had done previously. But, on paper, this week's price seemed too good to miss.

For a goal not to be scored within seven minutes of eight Premiership games meant that no goals were being forecast for 56 minutes of football (eight games multiplied by seven minutes). Strictly speaking, this had to be too high, though a series of weeks had produced remarkably late opening goals - including one in November where six Premiership matches were goalless until the 30th minute. Nevertheless, as we are quite confident that goals would be higher than recently, the first definite betting decision is to sell the time of the fastest goal for £30 per minute.

This roughly tallies with the staking plan for the day, as we think we have about a 1.5 minute advantage on the sell price - i.e our estimate for the time of the quickest goal is closer to five minutes. So our (very) theoretical profit is 1.5 points multiplied by the stake of £30 - or £45. This, when balanced with the rest of the day's betting activity, goes some way to producing our win target figure of £100.

Out of interest, we look at Stan James fixed-odds prices for the number of goals in each division and compare them to the spreads. One particular quote catches our attention. There are five games in the Scottish Premiership. Cantor Index have set their spread at 13.2-13.7, which we are tempted to buy. But Stan James have gone 11-8 that there are to be fewer than 14 goals. There is clearly a discrepancy. Of the three brackets priced by Stan James, the lowest is still only 0.2 lower than the sell-point of Cantor's quote. We are sure that it is the fixed-odds that are out of line, as experience has shown us that going low on Stan James' divisional goals bet is generally a good thing.

Towards kick-off time it starts to cloud over. We manage to do an about-turn on the goals theory, and though we have already sold the time of the fastest Premiership goal (which is a 'high goals' bet) decide to put £30 on 'under 14 goals' in the Scottish Premiership, simply on the basis that the price is screaming out to be backed. This, with a sudden change of tack, leads us to ditch the idea of buying other divisional goals completely, which leaves our total staking considerably below what we'd envisaged.

Instead we opt for a very small buy of IG's 'Goals Galore', advertised as available at 39. Here points are awarded on the basis of four points for any team in England scoring four goals, 10 for any team scoring five, 25 for six goals, 50 for seven and 100 for eight and above. The make-up of this market should be related to the overall number of goals that go in around the country, though not necessarily very closely.

Even if the goals per game are generally high, it doesn't necessarily mean that one or two teams will have posted a rugby score. However, in the past we had noted that the bet was scored in such a way as to reflect the general goal characteristics of an afternoon.

I've already decided to stick with some form of limited multiple bets with the individual team's fixed-odds selections, rather than trying to stake singles only. Being particularly confident that the FA Cup giant-killers would fall flat on their face, I want to stake proportionately more on them than the Premiership selections.

We opt to back those playing the giant-killers (Carlisle, Peterborough and Grimsby) in a series of eight lines, all staked to produce roughly the same win target (£140). So long as none of them actually lose, we will collect - as we are covering the different combinations of draws and wins. Seeing as Peterborough are as long as 11-2, this takes a fair amount of nerve, though Grimsby at 2-1 and Carlisle at 6-4 look safer territory.

We end up putting the four Premiership selections in with the giant-killers - including, after much debate, Bristol Rovers, even though they may have already experienced their come down following their FA Cup triumph the previous weekend. This forms a 'trebles from eight selections' bet to a total stake of £50. A separate £44 is placed on the series of eight trebles covering the three teams playing giant-killers.

Although you can plan in advance for the staking of fixed-odds bets, sometimes there has to be a very hasty adjustment to spread betting stakes, depending on the price you are given, which frequently is different from that advertised in the *Racing Post* or on Teletext. On ringing IG Index, the 39 we expect to get as the buy-point had transformed into 41, two points against us. When this happens we have developed a habit of shaving around 25 per cent off the intended stake, so in this case a small buy at £4 a point was trimmed to £3. The opposite case happened with the quote on the fastest Premiership goal. This was offered to sell at 7.5, half a point better than advertised, so the stake was upped to £35 a minute. Clearly this bet had a vast downside - a conceivable risk of over £250. But the total risk on the day was under £500, less than I would normally let run. This leaves us with a day's staking of:

**Sell**
**Fastest Premiership Goal for £35 at 7.5**

**Buy**
**'Goals Galore' at 41 for £3**

**Scottish Premiership Goals (under 14) £30 at 11-8**

**Any three from eight selections:**
**Aston Villa 1-2**
**Charlton 2-1**
**Everton 11-10**
**Leeds 8-5**
**Grimsby 2-1**
**Peterborough 4-1**
**Scunthorpe 7-4**
**Carlisle 6-4**

**£50 total**

**Any combination of draws and wins between**
**Grimsby 2-1**
**Peterborough 4-1**
**Carlisle 6-4**

**£45 total**

Overall, the prices obtained from Ladbrokes on the multiple bets were, across all selections, worse than competing companies, though I was determined that the bet should include the best price on Carlisle, who I feel are the strongest selection. With Ladbrokes best-priced at 6-4. I decide that I want to include this in the multiple bet, even at the expense of many other selections being available elsewhere at better prices. This is a major consideration you have to make when choosing with which company to place a multiple bet.

When watching the results come in, the usual pattern is to find a mixture of good and bad news, with some results in your favour and others against you. Only in the last 10 minutes before full-time does it really become clear whether the day is going to end in profit. However, with a stake on the fastest goal dwarfing the fixed-odds risks, we know that our fate for the day was to be sealed early.

I tend to follow the flow of goals on Sky's Soccer Saturday programme - slightly more entertaining than the traditional football gambler's habit of having to watch the scores pop up on the Ceefax service. The wait for the fastest goal is awful - one of the more excruciating spread betting experiences it's possible to suffer. Possibly the only naturally more uncomfortable bet is to sell total goal minutes in a live TV game.

Here the risk increases as the game goes on until, in stoppage-time, it reaches a something approaching more than the human mind can bear. I've never actually tried it - and I imagine that seeing as it is such an intrinsically nasty bet, there is probably a smattering of value to be had in being brave and going low.

But this afternoon, with an outrageous piece of good fortune, we hardly settle down in front of the box when news comes through that Alan Smith has scored for Leeds at Newcastle with a strike after 24 seconds - at that point the fastest goal of the Premiership season so far. With a profit of £227.50p already, we are close to assuring that the day would end in the black.

Even more unusually, two more goals go our way within the first five minutes. Carlisle go two up against Leyton Orient. In the Premiership, things are marginally in our favour, with Villa taking the lead at home to Derby, and Everton scoring against Sunderland. However, Leeds are soon pegged back and Charlton begin to sound like a lost cause at Blackburn.

Things look promising with the low goals bet in the Scottish Premiership, with the five games failing to produce a goal in the first 15 minutes. Elsewhere in the first-half, the goal tally remains above average, especially in the Premiership. But as the afternoon wears on the goals seem to dry up. At 4.00pm, only Carlisle, who have raced to a 4-0 lead in 45 minutes, are promising to contribute significantly to the 'Goals Galore' tally.

The biggest cheer is reserved for Peterborough taking the lead at Cardiff - otherwise, in terms of the bets, things remained quite static in the second-half.

With four out of the eight featuring in the multiple bet winning and nothing too scary going on with the three giant-killer selections, it is more a question of holding on to what we've got, rather than looking for things to go in our favour. With 15 minutes to go, a lot hinges on Grimsby hanging on at 0-0 against West Brom. With the other two selections safely ahead, it is the only result that could kill off the £45 stake.

Perilously late, 'Goals Galore' finally takes off, with four teams managing to get to four, and very late on, Carlisle hit a sixth against hapless Leyton Orient, resulting in a make-up of 45, a hard-earned £12 profit. With the Grimsby result coming through as 0-0, the wins/draws bet is in the bag as well. Overall, the set of trebles from eight doesn't break even, but the £30 on the Scottish Premiership goals bet really never gave us too many palpitations, with the division sputtering its way to just 11 goals

The final totting up on the kitchen table reveals a profit of £367.18p - for the stake level, a remarkably good afternoon's work. The profit already achieved has its usual effect on our attitude to betting on the live games on Sunday. Having eased to a figure well over a target for the purposes of this exercise, we take fright at all Sunday betting, quite irrationally. Our intention was to buy Arsenal's corner supremacy over Liverpool, on the grounds that Liverpool, for all their league position, had a very poor recent record of winning corners. But a price of 2-3 is enough to put us off; such is the degree of timidness that is engulfing us.

The theory that goals would be high turns out not to be true. Buying all the divisions, as originally planned, would have lost 11 points. The fact that 'Goals Galore' was profitable was very fortunate. Further study shows that buying 'Goals Galore' should be avoided in future, as it seems set permanently too high - possibly 20 per cent over the mathematically correct quote based on the last four season's results.

After profiting from the messy draws/wins bet, I am determined to use it more in future, as it often seems to be the case that I find exactly three selections that I want to back on any particular day. In the past I have tended to water these down with other selections to make up an 'any three from seven or eight' type of bet. But the option of backing just three teams to win or draw seems to concentrate the mind better.

For me, it is a rarity to make a profit figure of over £300 in a single day. Often I can study something endlessly during the week but end down on Saturday. My staking is not as consistent as it could be, borne out by the fact that my biggest individual loss was on, of all things, the Eurovision Song Contest (over £1,500), a spread bet which I had only considered to be a minimal risk. Oddly, my biggest individual win (of about an equal sum) was on the same event, two years earlier.

Although I don't have much time for those who are always concerned about 'minimising risk' - anyone worried about risk shouldn't be spread betting - there are situations where it is easy to suddenly lose a large sum without warning. With staking, you can slip into having a number of different bets on the same event' - almost by accident.

You can end up with a single selection propping up a number of multiple bets, or a feeling about how things will go - for instance, that there will be a lot of shocks in a round of FA Cup games. You then get into a one-dimensional way of thinking and start to back the same characteristic in a number of fixed-odds or spread bets. The danger is that if the fundamental characteristic of the afternoon doesn't happen, it can bring the whole pack of cards crashing down.

# postscript

While travelling through London recently, I had some time to kick my heels waiting for a train at Euston, so decided to pass the time reading the small print of the rules posted at William Hill in order to discover how they worded their stipulations regarding related bets. It was a week before the opening of the new Premiership season and all the company's coupons and posters had been redesigned, including their displayed rules sheet, presented in its customary tiny writing.

In amongst the general football rules there was a reference to a bet on 'team to score the first Premiership goal'. As far as I'm aware Hills have never offered this bet prior to the 2001-2002 season, so I assumed it was a new market that had yet to be unveiled. (By the time you are reading this the bet may have been available in the shops for a while.) Ten years ago I would have assumed that Hills' odds would perfectly reflect the true chances of each team scoring the first goal. But my experience since then, having looked at a mass of speciality bets, tends to make me think that they may struggle to post the correct odds.

Trying to work out the true percentages associated with the chance of each of 16-20 teams scoring the first goal is something of a mammoth task. You have to look at the forecast supremacy of one team over another, estimate the time of the first goal for each team, and then twist the whole calculation on its head before you even begin to emerge with reasonable estimates. Having not actually seen odds for this bet, my guess is that the strongest favourites will be offered at odds that are a touch too short, leaving the less obvious first scorers slightly on the long side.

This may all be wildly over-optimistic, but there is something to be said for having a positive mental attitude when betting on football. In gambling writing of the past, it was often gloomily said that "you never see a bookie going out of business". Well, we have now. The list of casualties in the betting industry grows ever longer. The gap between the amount of information that the odds compilers have access to and the amount we can lay our hands on, has become virtually non-existent.

In the battle between the bookie and the individual punter, there can be only one winner. But nowadays it is no longer clear who it will be.